UNITED NATIONS CONFERENCE ON TRADE AND DEVELOPMENT
Geneva

ECONOMIC DEVELOPMENT
IN AFRICA

Debt Sustainability:
Oasis or Mirage?

UNITED NATIONS
New York and Geneva, 2004

NOTE

Symbols of United Nations documents are composed of capital letters combined with figures. Mention of such a symbol indicates a reference to a United Nations document.

The designations employed and the presentation of the material in this publication do not imply the expression of any opinion whatsoever on the part of the Secretariat of the United Nations concerning the legal status of any country, territory, city or area, or of its authorities, or concerning the delimitation of its frontiers or boundaries.

Material in this publication may be freely quoted or reprinted, but acknowledgement is requested, together with a reference to the document number. A copy of the publication containing the quotation or reprint should be sent to the UNCTAD secretariat.

UNCTAD/GDS/AFRICA/2004/1

UNITED NATIONS PUBLICATION
Sales No. E.04.II.D.37
ISBN 92-1-112648-7

CONTENTS

Page

Introduction 1

Chapter I

Africa's debt overhang and HIPC debt relief: What are the issues? 3

1. Introduction 3

2. The genesis and nature of the African debt crisis 5

3. A brief history of debt relief 11

    (a) Traditional debt relief mechanisms 11

    (b) The HIPC Initiative 14

4. Issues arising in the implementation of the enhanced HIPC Initiative . 19

    (a) Pace of implementation 19

    (b) Long-term debt sustainability 20

    (c) Remaining on track post decision point 21

    (d) Interim relief 22

    (e) Financing 22

    (f) Creditor participation and "burden sharing" 24

    (g) "Additionality" 26

    (h) Pre-decision point and post-conflict countries 27

Chapter II

Analysis of eligibility and debt sustainability criteria of the HIPC Initiative 29

1. Introduction 29

2. Objectivity of HIPC eligibility criteria 29

    (a) The poverty criterion 29

    (b) Debt sustainability criteria 30

3. Examples of alternative debt sustainability criteria 43

4. Non-HIPC debt-distressed African countries 46

Chapter III

How sustainable is African HIPCs' debt after debt relief? 48

1. Post-HIPC debt sustainability 48

   (a) HIPC methodology to determine the amount of debt relief 50

   (b) Currency-specific short-term discount rates 54

2. Do HIPCs actually save on debt service? 55

   (a) NPV debt reductions lead to continuously high
      debt service payments 58

3. Is HIPC debt relief additional to traditional aid? 61

Chapter IV

New approaches to attaining sustainable debt levels 64

1. Introduction 64

2. Alternative modalities for delivering sustainable debt 64

   (a) Payment caps on HIPC debt service 64

   (b) The human development approach to debt sustainability 65

   (c) MDG-based approach to debt relief 66

3. Resource requirements 67

   (a) Requirements for attaining MDGs 67

   (b) Meeting the costs of a debt write-off 68

4. Addressing specific design problems in the HIPC Initiative 72

   (a) Revisions to HIPC eligibility and debt sustainability indicators 72

   (b) Overly optimistic growth projections 73

   (c) Insufficient interim debt relief 73

   (d) Adjustments in the burden-sharing concept 74

   (e) Using a single fixed low discount rate for the NPV calculation 75

Conclusions 76

Notes 78

References 85

List of Boxes

Box **Page**

1. Kenya: HIPC with "sustainable" debt 46

2. Nigeria: Non-HIPC debt-distressed African Country 47

List of Charts

Chart

1. Official, multilateral and private debt of Africa, 1970–2002 7

2. Africa's external debt situation, 1970–2002 10

3. HIPC Initiative: Breakdown of estimated potential costs by main creditors 23

4. Total debt service paid, 1990–2001 56

5. Total debt service paid to XGS, 1990–2001 57

6. Total debt service paid to GDP, 1990–2001 57

7. Projected debt service on public external debt, 2003–2005 59

8. Projected debt service on public external debt to projected exports, 2003–2005 60

9. Projected debt service on public external debt to projected government revenues, 2003–2005 60

List of Tables

Table

1. Africa's external debt ratios, 1970–2002 6

2. Paris Club restructuring terms for low-income countries, 1975–2001 .. 12

3. Eligibility thresholds: Original and enhanced HIPC 16

4. HIPC Initiative: Progress in implementation by country, status as of February 2004 18

5. HIPC Initiative: Estimates of costs to multilateral creditors and status of their commitments 25

6. HIPCs and other African countries: Comparisons based on per capita income, poverty (HPI-1) and IDA-only category 32

7. Selected debt indicators 34

List of Tables (contd.)

Table   **Page**

8. NPV debt-to-revenue ratios, with and without HIPC debt relief 38

9. Projections on public external debt service-to-government
   revenues, 2003–2005 39

10. Domestic public debt of African HIPCs: debt stock and interest
    payments, 2000–2002 41

11. Likelihood of achieving debt sustainability under
    different scenarios in 2020 49

12a Calculations of implicit growth rates for Government revenues,
    2003–2005 52

12b Calculations of implicit growth rates for exports, 2003–2005 53

13. Remaining debt of 27 HIPCs that reached the enhanced
    decision point by end-2003 69

Notes

- The $ sign refers to the US dollar.

- One billion equals one thousand million.

- One trillion equals one thousand billion.

Explanatory notes

Sub-Saharan Africa (SSA): Except where otherwise stated, this includes South Africa.

North Africa: Unlike in the UNCTAD *Handbook of Statistics*, in this publication Sudan is classified as part of sub-Saharan Africa, not North Africa.

Throughout, the term "dollar" ($) refers to US dollars, unless otherwise stated.

Abbreviations

AfDB	African Development Bank
CAFOD	Catholic Agency for Overseas Development
CIRR	commercial interest reference rate
COD	cut-off date
DSA	debt sustainability analysis
EURODAD	European Network on Debt and Development
FDI	foreign direct investment
FTAP	Fair and Transparent Arbitration Procedure
G-7	Group of Seven
GAO	General Accounting Office (of the United States)
GDI	gross domestic income
GDP	gross domestic product
GNI	gross national income
GNP	gross national product
HIPC	Heavily Indebted Poor Country (Initiative)
HIPCs	heavily indebted poor countries
HPI-1	Human Poverty Index for developing countries
IADB	Inter-American Development Bank
IBRD	International Bank for Reconstruction and Development
IDA	International Development Association
IMF	International Monetary Fund
KHS	Kenya shilling
MDB	multilateral development bank
MDG	Millennium Development Goal
NPV	net present value
ODA	official development assistance
OECD	Organisation for Economic Co-operation and Development
OED	Operations Evaluations Department (of the World Bank)
PC	Paris Club
PPG	public and publicly guaranteed
PRGF	Poverty Reduction and Growth Facility
PRSP	Poverty Reduction Strategy Paper
SDR	Special Drawing Rights
SDRM	Sovereign Debt Restructuring Mechanism
UK	United Kingdom
UNDP	United Nations Development Programme
US	United States of America
XGS	exports of goods and services

Introduction

In the context of the Millennium Development Goals (MDGs), the international community has set itself a target of reducing poverty by half by the year 2015. Many observers have now come to the conclusion that, on present trends, there is very little likelihood that this objective can be achieved at any time close to that date in the poorer countries, including in Africa.[1]

In its report on *Capital Flows and Growth in Africa* (UNCTAD, 2000), as in subsequent reports on economic development in Africa, UNCTAD has argued that the current levels of GDP growth would have to be raised to seven or eight per cent per annum and sustained if poverty reduction targets were to be met. This would imply doubling the current amount of aid to the continent and maintaining it at that level at least for a decade if the continent was to break the vicious circle of low growth and poverty. Such an action, within the context of an appropriate mix of domestic policies and supportive international measures, would generate sufficient investment and savings to reduce aid dependency in the longer term and place Africa on a sustainable growth path.

The continent's debt problems and its resource requirements are inextricably linked to the capacity of African countries to generate capital accumulation and growth. Among the policy measures that UNCTAD has advanced (UNCTAD, 1998) is the need for an independent assessment of debt sustainability in African countries by a high-level panel of experts on finance and development, selected jointly by debtors and creditors, with an undertaking by creditors to implement fully and swiftly any recommendations that might be made. While this recommendation did not find favour in the donor community, it was contended that the Heavily Indebted Poor Countries (HIPCs) Initiative, and later its enhanced version, would ensure a permanent exit solution to Africa's debt problems. There now seems to be an emerging consensus, however, that many African countries continue to suffer from a debt overhang despite the HIPC Initiative and various actions in the context of the Paris Club. The fact that even those countries that have reached (or are about to reach) the so-called completion point will soon find themselves in an unsustainable debt situation gives credence to the arguments advanced by critics with respect to the inappropriateness of the criteria applied in the debt sustainability analysis. And the fact that several more debt-distressed African countries are not eligible for HIPC debt relief reflects the lack of objectivity in the eligibility criteria.

Debt sustainability is basically a relative concept. The questions that beg for a response are: what level of debt is sustainable for countries in which the vast majority of the population lives on under $1 a day per person? Have debt sustainability criteria been based on internationally recognized benchmarks such as those of the MDGs, or on objectively and theoretically verifiable criteria? What is the relationship between Africa's total external debt stocks and the actual amount of debt serviced? Is complete debt write-off a moral hazard or a "moral imperative"?

The current study tries to put these and other related issues in perspective and makes a number of recommendations on how to deal with Africa's debt overhang, either through the adoption of new approaches or a major revision and improvement of present debt relief policies.

Chapter I

Africa's debt overhang and HIPC debt relief: What are the issues?

1. Introduction

The debt relief mechanisms launched in the late 1980s in the wake of the Latin American debt crisis addressed the commercial bank debt of middle-income developing countries. At the same time, in 1980, 56 per cent of Africa's total public and publicly guaranteed debt was official, and by 1995 the figure had increased to about 77 per cent. Corresponding ratios for multilateral debts were 14 per cent (1980) and 27 per cent (1995). Between 2000 and 2002, more than 80 per cent of Africa's public and publicly guaranteed debt was official, and about one third of it was multilateral debt.[2] Debt owed to multilateral financial institutions (MFIs) was considered immutable because of concerns with respect to the preferred creditor status of these institutions.

It was only in 1996 that the international financial community accepted the need for a comprehensive approach to the debt problems of the poorest low-income countries. The first major coordinated effort in this respect was the launch of the Heavily Indebted Poor Countries (HIPC) Initiative by the Bretton Woods Institutions (BWIs), the International Monetary Fund (IMF) and the World Bank. The Initiative was launched in response to concerns that many low-income countries would face unsustainable external public debt burdens even after receiving traditional debt relief. Against this background, the goal of the HIPC Initiative was to reduce the external public debt burden of all "eligible" heavily indebted poor countries (HIPCs) to sustainable levels in a reasonably short period of time. The Initiative was to make it possible for all HIPCs so designated to meet their "current and future external debt service obligations in full, without recourse to debt rescheduling or the accumulation of arrears, and without compromising growth" (IMF and World Bank, 2001a, p. 4).

An enhanced version of the HIPC Initiative was outlined in September 1999 after intensive pressures from non-governmental organizations (NGOs) and civil society at large, academics and debtor Governments highlighting the inadequacies of the Initiative. These include the limited country coverage of the original Initiative and the fact that it provided too little debt relief and delivery was too slow. The main aim of the enhanced HIPC Initiative is to strengthen the link between debt relief and policies tailored to a country's circumstances to reduce poverty through the delivery of "deeper, broader and faster" debt relief. Thus, the major modifications contained in the enhanced framework are larger reductions to total debt stock, faster reductions in debt-service payments and a relaxation of the stringent qualification criteria contained in the original HIPC Initiative.

Despite these improvements to the original Initiative, the enhanced HIPC has had its share of criticisms: "… progress has been much slower than expected and the Initiative is suffering from problems of underfunding, excessive conditionality, restrictions over eligibility, inadequate debt relief and cumbersome procedures" (United Nations, 2000, p. 2). The debt sustainability analysis (DSA) and the overly optimistic assumptions with respect to GDP and export growth rates have been particularly criticized. Also, estimates show that an increasing number of beneficiary countries are not likely to attain sustainable debt levels even after graduating from the Initiative. Regarding the eligibility criteria, it has been argued that eligibility ratios are based on a comprehensive measure of neither poverty nor indebtedness, and as a result neither the poorest nor the most indebted countries are HIPC-eligible. Poverty, it has been contended, is a multi-dimensional concept, and vulnerability factors are central to that concept, but they have been excluded from the HIPC approach (Dagdeviren and Weeks, 2001; Gunter, 2003; Drummond, 2004). The scope of country selection is regarded as too narrow, as the "IDA-only" criterion disqualifies some otherwise debt-strapped non-IDA countries (Gunter, 2001; G-24 Secretariat, 2003).[3] It has thus been asserted that political and cost factors were instrumental in setting the debt sustainability thresholds and eligibility criteria (Gunter, 2001; G-24 Secretariat, 2003).

Some analysts have also contended that any comprehensive debt sustainability analysis of low-income developing countries has to take account of domestic debt since it constitutes a large proportion of total public debt in some of the HIPCs and has the potential of impacting negatively on HIPCs' overall debt sustainability (Beaugrand, Loko and Mlachila, 2002; Fedelino and

Kudina, 2003). In addition, domestic debt has broad implications for government budgets, macroeconomic stability, private sector investment and overall economic growth performance (*Ibid.*; Chirwa and Mlachila, 2004; Debt Relief International, 2003).

2. The genesis and nature of the African debt crisis[4]

While private commercial bank lending accounts for much of the external debt of middle-income developing countries, most low-income African countries have borrowed more from multilateral financial institutions and official bilateral creditors. Such loans were directly contracted from other Governments or their export credit agencies (ECAs), and private loans were insured for payment by ECAs[5] (Daseking and Powell, 1999, p. 4). Indeed, in 1995 more than three-quarters of Africa's public and publicly guaranteed debt was official, and the continent's external debt crisis is therefore more of an "official" than a "commercial bank debt" crisis.

Africa's external debt burden increased significantly between 1970 and 1999. From just over $11 billion in 1970, Africa had accumulated over $120 billion of external debt in the midst of the external shocks of the early 1980s. Total external debt then worsened significantly during the period of structural adjustment in the 1980s and early 1990s, reaching a peak of about $340 billion in 1995, the year immediately preceding the launch of the original HIPC. Overall, Africa's external debt averaged $39 billion during the 1970s, before ballooning to just over $317 billion in the late 1990s. Over the same period, total debt service paid by the continent increased from about $3.5 billion to a peak of $26 billion (see table 1).

A major observation is that the continent's worsening external debt crisis was underscored by the ever-increasing levels of arrears, an indicator of the inability to service debt obligations on time. In 1995, for example, accumulated arrears on principal repayments had exceeded $41 billion, with countries in sub-Saharan Africa (SSA) owing almost all of this[6] and arrears representing one fifth of the total debt stock of SSA (see table 1). Secondly, there was a significant increase in the multilateral and official debt components of total outstanding debt during the 1980s and 1990s (see chart 1).

Table 1

AFRICA'S EXTERNAL DEBT RATIOS, 1970–2002
(Millions of dollars and percentages)

	1970–1979	1980–1989	1990–1999	1990–1996	1997–1999	2000–2002
	Average of period					
Africa						
Total debt stocks	39 270	180 456	303 232	297 191	317 325	292 561
Principal arrears	648	9 102	34 284	31 621	40 496	26 259
Total debt service paid	3 347	18 591	25 800	25 683	26 075	23 706
Total debt stocks / XGS	91.0	195.2	234.3	242.8	217.6	168.6
Total debt service paid / XGS	7.8	20.1	19.9	21.0	17.9	13.7
Principal arrears / XGS	1.5	9.8	26.5	25.8	27.8	15.1
Total debt stocks / GDP	24.2	51.7	65.3	67.0	61.8	54.6
Total debt service paid / GDP	2.1	5.3	5.6	5.8	5.1	4.4
Principal arrears / GDP	0.4	2.6	7.4	7.1	7.9	4.9
North Africa						
Total debt stocks	17 411	75 780	94 795	94 370	95 787	84 227
Principal arrears	46	3115	744	878	432	660
Total debt service paid	1 680	9 768	13 385	14 220	11 437	10 834
Total debt stocks / XGS	173.9	284.5	227.5	242.0	199.9	139.4
Total debt service paid / XGS	16.8	36.7	32.1	36.5	23.9	17.9
Principal arrears / XGS	0.5	11.7	1.8	2.3	0.9	1.1
Total debt stocks / GDP	44.3	68.1	60.9	65.8	51.8	40.3
Total debt service paid / GDP	4.3	8.8	8.6	9.9	6.2	5.2
Principal arrears / GDP	0.1	2.8	0.5	0.6	0.2	0.3
Sub-Saharan Africa						
Total debt stocks	21 859	104 676	208 436	202 821	221 539	208 334
Principal arrears	602	5 988	33 539	30 743	40 064	25 600
Total debt service paid	1 667	8 823	12 415	11 463	14 637	12 872
Total debt stocks / XGS	66.0	159.0	237.5	243.2	226.3	184.2
Total debt service paid / XGS	5.0	13.4	14.1	13.7	15.0	11.4
Principal arrears / XGS	1.8	9.1	38.2	36.9	40.9	22.6
Total debt stocks / GDP	17.7	44.0	67.5	67.6	67.4	63.7
Total debt service paid / GDP	1.4	3.7	4.0	3.8	4.5	3.9
Principal arrears / GDP	0.5	2.5	10.9	10.2	12.2	7.8

Source: UNCTAD secretariat computations based on World Bank, *Global Development Finance* and *World Development Indicators*, online data.

Note: XGS - exports of goods and services.

Chart 1

OFFICIAL, MULTILATERAL AND PRIVATE DEBT OF AFRICA, 1970–2002

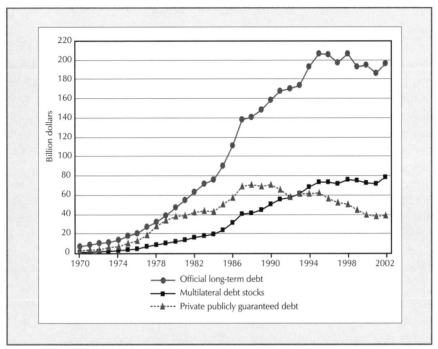

Source: UNCTAD secretariat computations based on World Bank, *Global Development Finance*, online data.

A significant factor in the debt crisis of African countries was the two oil price shocks of 1973–1974 and 1979–1980, the latter leading to a deterioration in the external environment that lasted until 1982. The rise in oil prices not only had an adverse impact on the trade balance of oil-importing countries, but also caused fiscal crises in most of these countries, thereby undermining domestic investment. The second shock occurred at a most inauspicious period, as it coincided with sharp rises in real interest rates. Within the context of the global recession of 1981–1982, which depressed demand for developing countries' exports, and deteriorating terms of trade, the balance of payments crisis that afflicted developing countries was exacerbated, not only for oil importers but also for oil exporters.   However, based on the assumption that the global recession would be short-lived and that prices of non-fuel commodities would recover quickly, most of these countries resorted to external borrowing to finance fiscal and external imbalances.

Some Asian countries with a strong manufacturing base chose to restrict the increase in their debt indicators by expanding export volume via a variety of export promotion measures and industrial policies. Many other developing countries did not adjust in this way, either because their economies were not sufficiently diversified or because they deliberately chose not to at the time (UNCTAD, 1988, p. 93; see also Balassa, 1981 and 1985; Kuznets, 1988). For many African countries, there was little room for manoeuvre not only because of their non-diversified economies, but mostly because of the steep decline in non-fuel primary commodity prices during the global recession of 1981–82. In sub-Saharan Africa, between 1980 and 1987, debt to GDP ratio rose from 38 per cent to 70 per cent, while the debt to export ratio rose from 150 per cent to 325 per cent. Per capita incomes fell by 14 per cent during the period.

Lending to low-income countries, particularly those in Africa, by bilateral and multilateral creditors was predicated on economic reforms being undertaken in the context of structural adjustment programmes, and total long-term outstanding debt increased by about 200 per cent between 1980 and 1995, the year before the HIPC Initiative was launched. The multilateral and official debt components increased by more than 500 per cent and 300 per cent respectively over the same period. The fact that these programmes failed to deliver on the promise of growth and development meant that the debt situation of many African countries continued to deteriorate.

Overall, the debt crisis in low-income developing countries, according to Brooks, et. al. (1998, pp. 4–10) and Daseking and Powell (1999, p. 5), could be traced to a combination of the following factors:

(i) Exogenous shocks (e.g. adverse terms of trade or bad weather), which affected highly commodity-dependent countries;

(ii) Lack of appropriate macroeconomic and structural policy response to such shocks;

(iii) Lending and refinancing by creditors, initially mostly on non-concessional terms (i.e. on commercial terms with short repayment periods), but from the 1980s shifting to concessional assistance and grants;

(iv) Imprudent debt management policies by borrowing countries, and use of loans on projects of doubtful viability, which undermined the capacity of countries to repay loans; and,

(v) Political factors such as wars and social strife in some borrowing countries.

A part of Africa's debt, particularly that of countries of geopolitical or strategic interest, is regarded by many as "odious", which raises the issue of the appropriate way to deal with the continent's debt crisis[7] (Vasquez, 2001, p. 10). For example, estimates show that, including imputed interest earnings, the accumulated stock of flight capital of Zaire (now the Democratic Republic of Congo) amounted to nearly $18 billion. The country's public external debt build-up thus appears to have been matched or exceeded by the accumulation of private external assets. Some evidence has been presented to the effect that the official and private creditors of the Mobutu regime knew, or should have known, that there was a high risk that their loans, or a substantial part of them, would not be used to benefit the Congolese people (see Ndikumana and Boyce, 1998).

A cursory glance at Africa's debt profile shows that the continent received some $540 billion in loans and paid back some $550 billion in principal and interest between 1970 and 2002. Yet Africa remained with a debt stock of $295 billion. For its part, SSA received $294 billion in disbursements and paid $268 billion in debt service, but remains with a debt stock of some $210 billion (chart 2). Discounting interest and interest on arrears, further payment of outstanding debt would represent a reverse transfer of resources.

That Africa's debt burden has been a major obstacle to the region's prospects for increased savings and investment, economic growth and poverty reduction cannot be denied. The continent's debt overhang has inhibited public investment in physical and social infrastructure. It has also hampered private investment, as investors could not be assured of policy continuity in an environment marked by severe external imbalances. And by undermining critical investments in health and human resource development, the debt overhang has compromised some of the essential conditions for sustainable economic growth, development, and poverty reduction. There is now a consensus that a permanent solution to the external debt crisis, along with increased official development assistance (ODA) and enhanced trade based on a level playing field, are critical to sustainable growth and development and to meeting the development challenges facing the African continent, including the Millennium Development Goals (MDGs), in particular that of halving poverty by 2015. Indeed, it is now generally agreed that the continent would need to at

Chart 2

AFRICA'S EXTERNAL DEBT SITUATION, **1970–2002**
(millions of dollars)

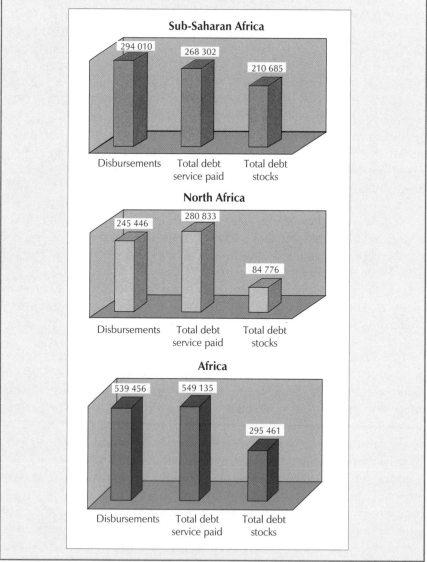

Sub-Saharan Africa

294 010

268 302

210 685

Disbursements   Total debt   Total debt
                 service paid   stocks

North Africa

245 446

280 833

84 776

Disbursements   Total debt   Total debt
                 service paid   stocks

Africa

539 456

549 135

295 461

Disbursements   Total debt   Total debt
                 service paid   stocks

Source: UNCTAD secretariat computations based on World Bank, *Global Development Finance*, online data.

Note: Total debt stocks at 2002.
          Cumulative disbursements and total debt service paid (1970–2002).

least double its rate of economic growth to some 7–8 per cent per annum and sustain this for about a decade in order to meet the MDGs.

3. A brief history of debt relief

(a) Traditional debt relief mechanisms

In the wake of the debt crisis of the middle-income countries of Latin America in the early 1980s, debt default was regarded as a major threat to the world banking system, which was ill prepared to absorb such losses (Daseking and Powell, 1999). Thus, initial attempts at the international level to address the debt burden, such as the Brady Plan (1989),[8] were focused on the commercial debt of middle-income developing countries. Generally, debt relief has been addressed within the framework of "traditional debt relief mechanisms", which include: concessional flow reschedulings, stock-of-debt operations, and bilateral forgiveness of ODA claims by the Paris Club; reschedulings and bilateral debt forgiveness by non-Paris Club official bilateral creditors; and private commercial debt relief and buy-back operations (Daseking and Powell, 1999, p.14)

For the low-income developing countries, debt relief has traditionally been provided within the context of the Paris Club through: rescheduling of principal and interest payments on either concessional or non-concessional terms, most often without any reduction in debt stocks; increasing concessionality, and/or write-offs, of bilateral ODA loans; and new concessional lending (see table 2). The commercial debt of this group of countries was reduced through the IDA's Debt Reduction Facility; while special programmes supported by bilateral donors were introduced to enable them to meet multilateral debt service obligations. For example, the "Fifth Dimension" programme was introduced in 1988 by the World Bank to enable IDA-only countries to repay interest on past IBRD loans; the IMF introduced the Rights Accumulation Programme in 1990 to enable countries to clear protracted arrears owed to it (for details, see UNCTAD, 1996, p. 49); and in 1997, the African Development Bank Group (AfDB) created a Supplementary Financing Mechanism, which became operational in 1998, as a quick-disbursing concessional assistance facility to help its member countries to meet interest payments on outstanding non-concessional loans (AfDB, 2000, p. 34).

Table 2

PARIS CLUB RESTRUCTURING TERMS FOR LOW-INCOME COUNTRIES, 1975–2001

Date/restructuring terms	Multilateral debt
1975-1998: Paris Club debt rescheduled but not cancelled or reduced in present value by reductions in interest.	Not applicable
October 1988: *Toronto Terms* under which, for the first time, bilateral debt can be reduced in net present value (NPV) terms by 33.3 per cent. This can be accomplished through a debt reduction or debt service reduction option.	Not reduced
December 1991: *London Terms* increased level of debt cancellation to 50 per cent of NPV of eligible debt service flows.	Not reduced
December 1994: *Naples Terms* raised level of debt reduction to 67 per cent of NPV of eligible debt service flows and/or stocks and set minimum debt reduction for "the poorest and most indebted countries" at 50 per cent of NPV. In September 1999, the 67 per cent threshold was applied to all heavily indebted poor countries.	Not reduced
December 1996: *Lyon Terms* (HIPC Initiative) raised debt reduction for heavily indebted poor countries to 80 per cent of NPV of eligible debt stock.	Debts owed to multilateral institutions (IMF, World Bank and regional develop-ment banks) may also be reduced. Concept of debt sustainability introduced.
November 1999: *Cologne Terms* (Enhanced HIPC Initiative) raised allowable debt reduction to 90 per cent of NPV, or more, of eligible debt stock "if necessary to achieve sustainability in the framework of the HIPC Initiative".	Debts of bilateral and multi-lateral official creditors to be reduced sufficiently to attain debt sustainability as defined by the Initiative.

Source: Adapted from Sachs (2002), box 1, pp. 276–277, and UNCTAD sources.

Notes: 1. Dates in Table refer to when the Paris Club officially approved the Terms and are therefore different from the dates (used in the text) on which they were approved by the G8.

      2. At its Meeting in October 2003 in Evian, France, the G8 endorsed a new approach, which focuses on long-term debt sustainability for non-HIPCs. The "Evian approach", as it became known, emphasizes more flexibility in dealing with external debt crisis and more willingness to reduce the debt of countries, which are at risk, or display the signs, of insolvency.

The implementation of Paris Club debt relief is underscored by a set of five principles. Decisions are taken on a case-by-case basis to facilitate permanent adjustment to the specificities of each debtor country, and they are based on consensus. The debtor country must have an appropriate programme supported by the IMF to demonstrate the need for debt relief. In addition, all creditors must agree to implement the terms agreed in the context of the Paris Club, which preserves comparability of treatment between different creditors.[9]

Prior to the introduction of the HIPC Initiative, the debt eligible for rescheduling in the Paris Club comprised all medium- and long-term debt, both public and publicly guaranteed, contracted under ODA and non-ODA terms. In the vast majority of cases, debts contracted after the post cut-off date and short-term loans (under one year) were not eligible for rescheduling, although there are some exceptional cases where the Paris Club included such debts in the rescheduling package.[10] In the context of the HIPC Initiative, it became increasingly clear that limiting eligible debt to pre-cut-off date debts was too restrictive, as a number of countries would not reach sustainability thresholds unless post cut-off date debts were also included in the debt cancellation package. Hence, the Paris Club now applies flexibility with regard to the cut-off date.

Since the early signs of the debt crisis in the mid-1970s, UNCTAD has consistently provided in-depth analysis of the debt problems of developing countries and of the urgent need to resolve the debt overhang. Indeed the first major coordinated action of the international community to deal with the debt overhang of the poorest low-income developing countries was taken within the context of resolution 165 S-IX (1978)[11] adopted by UNCTAD's Trade and Development Board in 1978, which translated into debt forgiveness to the tune of some US$ 6 billion for poor countries. Research by the UNCTAD secretariat in the mid to late 1990s continued to emphasize the importance of finding a lasting solution that would address both long-term and immediate needs of debtor countries, and highlighted the fact that, in the long-term, sufficient development finance must be provided on terms and levels consistent with their development needs. In the case of heavily indebted poor countries with an unsustainable debt burden, UNCTAD underscored as early as 1988 the inadequacy of existing schemes to deal with their critical situation and the need for innovative mechanisms to deal with the debt overhang of the poorer countries (UNCTAD, 1988, in particular chapter IV, pp. 120–122; see also UNCTAD, 1996, pp. 55–57;).

(b) The HIPC Initiative

As mentioned earlier, in 1995 multilateral debt comprised about a quarter of the total long-term outstanding debt of Africa, more than double its share in 1980 (chart 1). The HIPC Initiative was a unique debt relief package compared to the traditional debt relief approaches, as it sought to reduce debt stocks to sustainable levels subject to satisfactory policy performance of beneficiaries, while situating debt relief within a framework of poverty reduction. It was expected to be a comprehensive debt relief framework dealing with the debt problems of some of the world's poorest countries, and being the only relief package that addressed the issue of multilateral debt and attempted to involve all stakeholders — debtor Governments, commercial creditors and the donor community — the initiative also benefited from a remarkable advocacy effort by civil society.

Only the poorest developing countries, most of them from Africa, were eligible for debt relief under the Initiative. This group of countries was defined as (i) "those that are only eligible for highly concessional assistance from the International Development Association (IDA) and from the IMF's Poverty Reduction and Growth Facility", and (ii) "those that also face an unsustainable debt situation even after the full application of traditional debt relief mechanisms (such as application of Naples terms under the Paris Club agreement)".[12] Finally, a country became fully eligible only after successfully implementing macroeconomic stabilization and policy reforms for a period of three years, whereby it reached the decision point. The latter refers to a process in which the Boards of the IMF and World Bank formally approved a country's eligibility and the international community committed itself to providing the debt relief required to reach debt sustainability, provided policy reforms remained on track over the following three years. Thus, a six-year good track record was required for full eligibility (i.e. reaching completion point) and commitment by the international community to provide "irrevocable" debt relief under the original HIPC.[13]

The original Initiative defined a country's debt situation as being sustainable as long as selected debt ratios were within certain thresholds after a debt sustainability analysis (DSA) was undertaken by the staff of the IMF and the World Bank and officials of the debtor country. These thresholds were defined in the following manner: first, the ratio of the net present value (NPV)[14] of a country's external public and publicly guaranteed (PPG) debt to exports of goods and non-factor services must be within a range of 200 to 250 per cent; second, the debt service on PPG external debt to exports ratio must be within a range of 20 to 25 per cent. The exact ratios within these two ranges were determined by using country-specific vulnerability factors. The key vulnerability factors were based on a country's GDP per capita level and export concentration. At least in the early cases, the debt service criterion was a less-binding one, and debt sustainability analyses therefore centred more on the NPV debt-to-export ratio.

The Initiative also stipulated that for very open economies, where exclusive reliance on external indicators might not adequately reflect the fiscal burden of external debt, a country with an NPV debt-to-export target below the 200–250 per cent range could be recommended if it met two minimum threshold requirements: an export-to-GDP ratio of 40 per cent, and a fiscal-revenues-to-GDP ratio of 20 per cent. For countries meeting both of these thresholds, instead of the standard NPV debt-to-export target, a different target was set whereby the NPV of debt would be 280 per cent of fiscal revenues. Bolivia, Burkina Faso, Mali, Mozambique and Uganda qualified under the export criterion of the original framework. Côte d'Ivoire and Guyana qualified under the NPV debt-to-revenue criterion, which is also called the HIPC Initiative's "fiscal window".

Three years after its launch in 1999, it had become evident that the Initiative was not sufficient to provide HIPCs with a permanent exit from repeated debt rescheduling, nor did it provide enough resources to deal with the pressing challenges of poverty reduction. Concerns were expressed about the limited country coverage of the Initiative and the fact that it provided too little debt relief and delivery was too slow. In addition, even with debt relief under the Initiative, beneficiary countries were spending much more on debt servicing than on public health and education. In the light of these concerns and increasing public pressure, including from NGOs and civil society at large, academics, and some HIPC Governments, all of which highlighted the inadequacies of the original Initiative, the IMF and the World Bank formally agreed to an enhanced version of the Initiative in September 1999. The main aim of the enhanced HIPC Initiative was to strengthen the link between debt relief and policies tailored to a country's circumstances in order to reduce poverty through the delivery of "deeper, broader and faster" debt relief.

The enhanced framework lowered the ratio of NPV of debt to exports to a fixed ratio of 150 per cent (replacing the previous range of 200–250 per cent). It also lowered the minimum thresholds for the "fiscal window" to an export-to-GDP ratio of at least 30 per cent (previously 40 per cent) and a revenue-to-GDP ratio of 15 per cent (previously 20 per cent). For countries meeting these new thresholds, the NPV debt-to-revenue ratio was lowered from 280 per cent to 250 per cent (see table 3). It was estimated that, due to these changes in the enhanced HIPC debt sustainability definitions, seven additional countries, five of them in Africa (Benin, Central African Republic, Ghana, Honduras, Lao People's Democratic Republic, Senegal and Togo), would become eligible for HIPC debt relief.[15]

A major enhancement is the "frontloading" of debt relief, that is the provision of a proportion of debt relief to eligible countries at the decision point in order to maximize support for poverty reduction programmes. The enhanced HIPC is retroactive in that it reassesses countries that had already qualified under the original HIPC framework for additional relief based on the revised eligibility benchmarks. It also introduces a "floating completion point", whereby the completion point is no longer fixed at the end of three years (after the decision point), but is allowed to "float" in line with the pace of each country's reform. Thus, the assessment of a country's performance during the interim period is based on specific outcomes of policy reforms agreed at the decision point; the maintenance of macroeconomic stability; and the implementation of a PRSP (poverty reduction strategy paper)[16] for at least one year, rather than the

Table 3

ELIGIBILITY THRESHOLDS: ORIGINAL AND ENHANCED HIPC

Element	Original	Enhanced
NPV debt-to-export ratio (%)	200 to 250	150
NPV debt-to-revenue ratio (%)	280	250
Openness criterion (exports as a % of GDP)	40	30
Revenue threshold (revenue as a % of GDP)	20	15
Debt relief	Fixed at completion point	Interim relief at decision point
Front-loading of debt relief	No	Yes

Source: Gautam (2003).

length of the track record. A country reaches the completion point once these criteria are met, and the international community commits itself to providing irrevocable debt relief (agreed at the decision point, or with a top-up, if circumstances justify) to enable the country to reach the so-called sustainable debt levels.

In general, the HIPC Initiative supplements traditional debt relief mechanisms with new debt relief grants. It is governed by the principle of "equitable burden sharing", with each multilateral creditor, donor agency and commercial creditor providing debt relief proportional to the amount of a country's indebtedness to it after full application of traditional debt relief mechanisms. Furthermore, the Initiative ensures that steps taken by MFIs are in line with their status as "preferred creditors"; in the event of default or external debt servicing problems, sovereign borrowers make preferential allocation of foreign exchange to service the debts owed to these institutions without triggering remedial action on the part of the other creditors. However, a problem remains in that the failure of HIPCs to meet their debt service obligations could lead to the suspension of debt rescheduling agreements and/or cessation of new financial flows from the participating creditor institutions.

Judging by the current composition of the HIPC group, the problem of external debt overhang in the poorest countries appears to be mainly an African problem, which is probably not too surprising considering that 34 of the 50 least developed countries (LDCs), as defined by the United Nations, are African. Of the 42 HIPC-eligible countries worldwide, 34 are in Africa, 4 in Latin America and 4 in Asia. The external debts of four of these countries (Angola, Kenya, Viet Nam and Yemen) have been judged to be potentially sustainable. As at the end of February 2004, 23 African countries had reached their decision points, and seven of these were at their completion points (see table 4). In all, the total estimated costs of the Initiative have increased from $12.5 billion (in 1998 NPV terms) for 29 countries to $39.4 billion (in 2002 NPV terms) for 34 countries.

Table 4

HIPC Initiative: Progress in implementation by country,
status as of February 2004

	Decision point date	Completion point date
Completion point		
Benin	July 2000	April 2003
Bolivia	*February 2000*	*June 2001*
Burkina Faso	July 2000	April 2002
Mali	September 2000	February 2003
Mauritania	February 2000	June 2002
Mozambique	April 2000	September 2001
Uganda	February 2000	May 2000
United Republic of Tanzania	April 2000	November 2001
Decision point		
Cameroon	October 2000	Floating
Chad	May 2001	Floating
Congo	July 2003	Floating
Ethiopia	November 2001	Floating
Gambia	December 2000	Floating
Ghana*	February 2002	Floating
Guinea	December 2000	Floating
Guinea-Bissau	December 2000	Floating
Guyana	*November 2000*	*Floating*
Honduras	*July 2000*	*Floating*
Madagascar	December 2000	Floating
Malawi	December 2000	Floating
Nicaragua	*December 2000*	*Floating*
Niger*	December 2000	Floating
Rwanda	December 2000	Floating
Sao Tome and Principe	December 2000	Floating
Senegal	June 2000	Floating
Sierra Leone	March 2002	Floating
Zambia	December 2000	Floating

Source: IMF and the World Bank, *Heavily Indebted Poor Countries (HIPC) Initiative – Statistical Update, 2004*, annex II, pp. 9–10.

Note: Countries in italics are non-African countries.
*   * Niger and Ghana have since reached their completion points — in April and July 2004, respectively.

4. Issues arising in the implementation of the enhanced HIPC Initiative

The history of implementation of the Initiative to date has highlighted several challenges that might yet detract from its limited success. One problem that has dogged the Initiative since its introduction in 1996 is its slow pace. Equally serious problems have surfaced recently, which include: difficulties in maintaining longer-term debt sustainability; HIPCs getting off track following the decision point; insufficiency of interim relief; financing problems; lack of full creditor participation; doubtful "additionality"; and pre-decision (and post-conflict) cases.

(a) Pace of implementation

The implementation of the original Initiative was slow until the adoption of the enhanced framework in the last quarter of 1999, and it has slowed down once again since December 2000. In the first three years following its launch (fall 1996 until fall 1999), only six HIPCs (Bolivia, Burkina Faso, Côte d'Ivoire, Mali, Mozambique and Uganda) reached the decision point. After the adoption of the enhanced framework in the fall of 1999, there was a commitment by various donor Governments and international organizations to the effect that at least 20 HIPCs should receive some debt relief under the Initiative by the end of 2000. In fact, 22 HIPCs reached their enhanced decision points by the end of December 2000. However, progress has slackened since then, and only five HIPCs (Chad, the Democratic Republic of Congo, Ethiopia, Ghana and Sierra Leone) have reached the enhanced decision point within the last three years (January 2001 to January 2004).

Moreover, while the enhanced framework was adopted with the expectation that HIPCs that had reached their enhanced decision points would reach their enhanced (floating) completion points within less than three years, all of the 12 HIPCs that reached their enhanced decision point between October and December 2000 (Cameroon, the Gambia, Guinea, Guinea-Bissau, Guyana, Madagascar, Malawi, Nicaragua, Niger, Rwanda, Sao Tome and Principe, and Zambia) failed to reach the enhanced completion point by December 2003 (see table 4). Nicaragua and Niger reached their enhanced completion point in January 2004 and April 2004 respectively. Ethiopia and

Ghana, which reached their enhanced decision point in November 2001 and February 2002, also reached their enhanced completion point in April 2004 and July 2004 respectively.

Specific measures to be undertaken before the completion point is reached have also been implemented with varying degrees of success. These include preparation of Poverty Reduction Strategy Papers (PRSPs) and implementation of Poverty Reduction and Growth Facility (PRGF) programmes which have been delayed in many cases. According to the IMF and the World Bank, protracted interruptions — due to political tensions, fiscal policy slippages and weak governance in the area of public resource management — have characterized the implementation of policy reform in several HIPCs, notably Guinea-Bissau, Malawi and Sao Tome and Principe. Other countries, such as Cameroon, the Gambia, Guinea and Zambia, have experienced problems in programme implementation (IMF and World Bank, 2003a, pp. 15–23).[17]

(b) Long-term debt sustainability

It is becoming increasingly doubtful whether HIPC Initiative beneficiaries could attain sustainable debt levels after reaching the completion point and maintain these levels in the long term. In April 2001 the IMF and World Bank (2001a) issued a paper that recognized for the first time that the HIPC Initiative might not achieve long-term debt sustainability. The DSA is based on medium-term economic projections developed by the IMF and the World Bank. One important aspect of this analysis involves ascertaining whether the export and revenue criteria are met. In the case of the export criteria, the average level of exports for the most recent three-year period is used as a benchmark, while the revenue figures are based on an average of Government's fiscal accounts in the three years preceding the cut-off date. Depending on the cut-off date for computing debt relief, the prices and volumes of the major exports of a country in the most recent three-year period could have a great impact on whether a country's debt is deemed sustainable or not. Similarly, owing to the commodity dependence of poor African countries (see UNCTAD, 2003), a significant deviation of commodity prices from the levels projected in the DSA could bias conclusions about HIPC debt sustainability. For example, when the debt crisis began in the early 1980s, Latin American debt was deemed sustainable on the basis of the results of models that failed to take account of the possibility of a sharp drop in commodity prices during the mid-1980s (Cline, cited in

Claessens, et al., 1996), just as current projections on debt sustainability did not take account of the recent significant drop in coffee and cotton prices.

According to the IMF and the World Bank's own analysis, some completion point countries (notably Uganda) currently have debt ratios exceeding sustainable levels as defined by the Initiative. There are various reasons for this, including the drastic fall in commodity prices from the late 1990s to the end of 2002, over-optimistic assumptions for economic and export growth, and in some cases new borrowings (IMF and World Bank, 2002a). For example, the World Bank's Operations Evaluation Department (OED) Review reveals that, "the overall simple average of the growth rate assumed in DSAs …is more than twice the historical average for 1990–2000, and almost six times the average for 1980–2000" (Gautam, 2003, p. 28). This highlights the difficulties involved in attaining sustainable debt levels as defined by the Initiative.

Growth is critical for both debt sustainability and poverty reduction. However, the Initiative currently places heavy emphasis on social expenditures as the primary means of poverty reduction on the assumption that macroeconomic policies contained in the PRSPs will lead to growth. UNCTAD had earlier cautioned that where there are trade-offs between public spending in priority and non-priority areas, these should be scrutinized from the view point of their overall impact on growth, and that in the African context, high and rising levels of public investment, particularly in infrastructure, are essential for moving into a sustained growth process (UNCTAD, 2002a, p. 26). Indeed, the need for the performance criteria to be balanced between growth-enhancing and social expenditure priorities and tailored to individual country circumstances has been identified in the OED report on HIPC (Gautam, 2003). A more recent OED report evaluating the poverty reduction strategy initiative corroborates many of the findings of UNCTAD with respect to the weaknesses of the PRSP process (World Bank 2004b). In the light of the possible adverse macroeconomic impact of domestic debt (see chapter 2), the possibility of HIPCs attaining sustainable high rates of growth consonant with long-term debt sustainability and poverty reduction is likely to be overestimated.

(c) Remaining on track post decision point

Remaining on track with economic reforms and poverty reduction programmes during the interim period (i.e. for countries already past their decision point but not yet at completion point) has proven to be difficult and has caused delays in bringing to completion point some of the HIPCs that reached the decision point since at the end of 2000 (as discussed above).

An integral part of this problem is the challenge of maintaining macroeconomic stability and the preparation of a full PRSP, which is a major requirement in the enhanced Initiative, the prime objective being to link debt relief resources with the promotion of poverty reduction. Finalization of interim PRSPs has proved particularly daunting.[18] Full engagement of all stakeholders in the participatory process, data collection and analysis, establishing priority objectives and sectoral strategies, and costing have taken much longer than expected. Furthermore, difficulties in establishing public expenditure management systems and transparent mechanisms for monitoring debt relief spending, and the paucity of institutional and human resource capacity, have militated against the timely preparation of PRSPs (IMF and World Bank, 2003a, pp. 15–22).

(d) Interim relief

While the provision of interim debt relief is almost certainly an improvement over the original HIPC, the amount of interim assistance does not appear to be sufficient to meet poverty reduction needs in the critical phase of the programme. Under the current arrangements, the IMF could disburse up to 60 per cent of total debt relief as interim relief. The World Bank and the AfDB could disburse up to 33 per cent and 40 per cent respectively.[19] However, the AfDB had not met this target in a single case at the end of 2003. Non-Paris Club bilateral creditors typically provide flow rescheduling on Cologne terms, although it is generally agreed that "front loading" debt relief (i.e. providing interim relief) is crucial for the poverty reducing programmes of HIPCs.

(e) Financing

Financing the total cost of the Initiative has been problematic. Under the enhanced Initiative, total estimates for debt relief for 34 HIPCs as of September 2003 were $39.4 billion (in 2002 NPV terms). Multilateral creditors are to account for about $19 billion (48 per cent), while bilateral and commercial creditors together are to account for the remaining $20.4 billion (52 per cent).[20] (See chart 3 for the breakdown of the costs to major multilateral creditors).

Chart 3

HIPC INITIATIVE: BREAKDOWN OF ESTIMATED POTENTIAL COSTS BY MAIN CREDITORS
(2002 NPV terms)

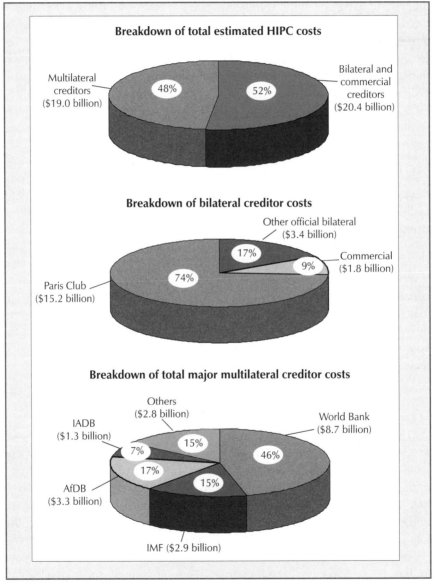

Breakdown of total estimated HIPC costs

Multilateral creditors ($19.0 billion) — 48%

52% — Bilateral and commercial creditors ($20.4 billion)

Breakdown of bilateral creditor costs

Other official bilateral ($3.4 billion) — 17%

9% — Commercial ($1.8 billion)

Paris Club ($15.2 billion) — 74%

Breakdown of total major multilateral creditor costs

Others ($2.8 billion) — 15%

IADB ($1.3 billion) — 7%

AfDB ($3.3 billion) — 17%

IMF ($2.9 billion) — 15%

World Bank ($8.7 billion) — 46%

Source: IMF and World Bank (2003a).

To date, resources covering the total estimated costs of the Initiative have yet to be secured, and the problem is likely to be aggravated if estimates are included for post-conflict countries (for which there are no current estimates) and for "topping up" at the completion point. Preliminary calculations suggest that the cost of HIPC debt relief could increase by more than 25 per cent (or by $10.6 billion to $50.0 billion in 2002 NPV terms) if the costs of providing relief to Sudan, Liberia, Somalia and Lao People's Democratic Republic are taken into account. In addition, about $729 million would be required for topping up (IMF and World Bank, 2003a, pp. 14–15). The latter figure, however, is likely to have been grossly underestimated if, as accepted by the Bretton Woods institutions, their own estimates for calculating debt sustainability levels are over-optimistic.

Most of the multilateral development banks' debt relief (and even some of the IMF's) is actually financed by bilateral donors, partly through contributions to the HIPC Trust Fund (hereafter, the Trust Fund) and partly through direct contributions to MFIs in the form of replenishments (like IDA replenishments).[21]

Most regional development banks from the South, including the AfDB, face severe financing constraints. For most of them, debt relief would almost certainly be financed through the Trust Fund. As at September 2002, eight regional development banks had used the Trust Fund to help them in the delivery of their share of HIPC debt relief, and several others had also approached the Fund for possible financial support to enable them to provide their share (IMF and World Bank, 2002b, p. 17).[22]

(f) Creditor participation and "burden sharing"

The DSA assumes that all creditors will provide HIPC assistance proportional to their share of the debt after the full application of traditional forms of debt relief. However, while the Initiative has certainly witnessed a marked increase in the number of creditors participating in it, not all creditors are participating fully as expected, nor have they indicated their willingness to do so. As of June 2003, at least 37 bilateral creditors had not agreed to deliver some or all of the required HIPC debt relief. Based on initiated litigations, there is also some indication that a significant share of commercial creditors might not participate in the HIPC Initiative.[23] Furthermore, there are about seven multilateral creditors that have not indicated their intention to provide debt relief under the Initiative (see table 5).

Table 5

HIPC INITIATIVE: ESTIMATES OF COSTS TO MULTILATERAL CREDITORS
AND STATUS OF THEIR COMMITMENTS
(Costs in millions of dollars, in 2002 NPV terms)

Creditor	Cost of providing HIPC debt relief *(for 27 countries)*	Cost of providing HIPC debt relief *(for 34 countries)*	% increase in costs *(from 27 to 34 countries)*
Delivering or committed to delivering debt relief	**16 769**	**18 938**	**12.9**
World Bank Group	7 700	8 742	13.5
International Monetary Fund (IMF)	2 677	2 935	9.6
African Development Bank (AfDB)	2 772	3 297	18.9
Inter-American Development Bank (IADB)	1 250	1 250	0.0
Central American Bank for Economic Integration (CABEI)	565	565	0.0
European Union/European Investment Bank (EU/EIB)	663	773	16.6
International Fund for Agricultural Development (IFAD)	268	294	9.7
Arab Bank for Economic Development in Africa (BADEA)	187	230	23.0
OPEC Fund for International Development	160	185	15.6
Islamic Development Bank (IsDB)	136	144	5.9
Corporacion Andina de Fomento (CAF)	106	106	0.0
Arab Fund for Social and Economic Development (AFESD)	71	71	0.0
Caricom Multilateral Clearing Facility (CMCF)	66	66	0.0
West African Development Bank (BOAD)	47	70	48.9
Fund for the Financial Development of the River Plate Basin (FONPLATA)	28	28	0.0
Nordic Development Fund (NDF)	25	25	0.0
Caribbean Development Bank (CDB)	20	20	0.0
Arab Monetary Fund (AMF)	13	13	0.0
Central Bank for West African States (BCEAO)	6	37	516.7
Nordic Investment Bank (NIB)	4	4	0.0
East African Developement Bank (EADB)	4	4	0.0
Banque des Etats de l'Afrique Centrale (BDEAC)	1	4	300.0
Asian Development Bank (AsDB)	0	75	n.a
Have not indicated intention to provide relief under the HIPC Initiative	**71**	**73**	**2.8**
Banque des Etats de l'Afrique Centrale (BEAC)	35	35	0.0
Economic Community of West African States (ECOWAS)	15	16	6.7
Eastern and Southern African Trade and Development Bank (PTA Bank)	9	9	0.0
Banque de Dévelopment des Etats des Grands Lacs (BDEGL)	6	6	0.0
Conseil de L'Entente (FEGECE)	3	4	33.3
Fondo Centroamericano de Estabilizacion Monetaria (FOCEM)	2	2	0.0
Fund for Solidarity and Economic Development (FSID)	1	1	0.0
Total	**16 840**	**19 011**	**12.9**

Source: IMF and World Bank (2003a).

Although the overall share of these non-participating creditors in total HIPC debt relief costs is relatively small (at most 5 per cent), the costs to individual HIPCs could be high. Also, in cases where non-participating creditors have sued to recover debts, costs to HIPCs could be significant. Uganda, for example, has incurred a fine of $28.9 million in interest charges and legal fees to be paid to five creditors that have initiated legal action to recover debts — Iraq and commercial creditors from Spain, the United Kingdom and the former Yugoslavia (IMF and the World Bank, 2003b). Creditor litigations[24] have arisen due to various shortcomings in the HIPC Initiative:

(i) The Initiative does not constitute international law, and thus HIPCs are obliged to pay their debt service in full until individual agreements have been signed with each creditor;

(ii) Some creditors are formally or de facto excluded from the decision-making process;[25]

(iii) No provision has been made to exempt creditors that are themselves HIPCs from the burden sharing of the HIPC Initiative; and,

(iv) In contradiction with existing Paris Club regulations, there is no "de minimis" clause (which would have exempted minor creditors from providing HIPC debt relief) for non-Paris Club creditors participating in the HIPC Initiative.

In part, the lack of full participation by creditors is also due to the fact that though non-Paris Club creditors are to provide debt relief commensurate with that delivered by the MFIs, there is no well-defined framework for this. The current approach for securing debt relief by HIPCs from these creditors could, at best, be described as based primarily on moral suasion.[26]

(g) "Additionality"

Dovetailing with the above is the issue of whether the Initiative satisfies one of its core principles of "additionality", that is each dollar of debt relief should be additional to existing aid. The issue is particularly troubling as the World Bank's OED Report concludes that there has been close to zero overall additionality, although most recent trends in aid flows indicate some aid reallocations towards eligible HIPCs (Gautam, 2003). The World Bank argues that it is impossible to answer conclusively by looking at data whether HIPC debt relief is additional because of the problem of the counterfactual. Nevertheless, it concludes that: "All in all, the available data indicate a modest rise in total aid resources to HIPCs during the period of the Initiative." (World Bank, 2003, box 6.2, p. 135)

(h) Pre-decision point and post-conflict countries

Notwithstanding all the above-mentioned implementation issues, it is the pre-decision point and/or post-conflict countries that might prove to be the Achilles' heel of the Initiative. While the 2004 Spring Summit of the G8 at Sea Island (United States) suggested a top-up of funding for the Initiative and an extension of the sunset clause by two more years to end-December 2006, it is not yet clear how soon this top-up would be available and whether it would be enough to cover the costs of debt relief for all pre-decision point countries. As discussed above, current cost estimates do not include the cost of debt relief to some of these countries. Pre-decision point countries are those eligible countries that have yet to be considered for assistance — i.e. they have not yet reached their decision points. Eleven countries fell into this category as at June 2003, with Lao People's Democratic Republic and Myanmar being the only non-African countries in the list.[27] Almost all of these countries are conflict-affected, are still in conflict, or are just emerging from conflict; and a few have huge arrears that would have to be settled before the decision point is reached.

Resurgence of domestic conflicts disrupted the stabilization programmes in Burundi, Central African Republic and Côte d'Ivoire. In the case of Côte d'Ivoire, political crisis in the third quarter of 2002 interrupted progress toward reaching the decision point under the enhanced Initiative. Lack of political consensus on issues such as revenue sharing prevented the Comoros from reaching its decision point. Elsewhere, a lack of effective implementation of economic and financial policies has been a key impediment in reaching the decision point (IMF and World Bank, 2003a). Some counties have also not been able to reach the decision point because of protracted arrears and/or conflicts (Liberia, Somalia and Sudan). A special financing arrangement had to be put in place by the African Development Bank (AfDB), with the support of the World Bank, before the Democratic Republic of Congo could reach its decision point (AfDB Annual Report, 2002; and World Bank, 2003, p. 142),[28] and Guinea-Bissau and Niger had to receive bilateral assistance to clear their arrears to the AfDB in order to get to the decision point.

At another level, the design of the Initiative has been criticised by various commentators and some HIPC Governments for the arbitrary use of discount rates to calculate the NPV of debt, which determines the volume of debt relief for each beneficiary, the narrowness of the eligibility criteria, which exclude some poor debt-distressed countries, the use of unrealistic debt sustainability criteria, and the exclusion of domestic debt in determining debt sustainability thresholds. The next chapter takes up some of the criticisms of the design of the Initiative.

Chapter II

Analysis of eligibility and debt sustainability criteria of the HIPC Initiative

1. Introduction

There is growing criticism that the HIPC eligibility criteria, defined in terms of NPV debt-to-exports ratios and thresholds for fiscal sustainability are arbitrary, lacking in objectivity, and based on debt relief costs to creditors instead of the debt relief needs of HIPCs for their sustainable development. The exclusion of vulnerability factors in these criteria has also led to a narrow definition of poverty and indebtedness (Dagdeviren and Weeks, 2001; Sachs, 2002; Gunter, 2003; Drummond, 2004). Sachs, for example, has argued that official creditors (the Paris Club and multilateral creditors like the IMF and the World Bank) "have used arbitrary formulas rather than a serious analysis of country needs to decide on the level of debt relief... [consequently] the so-called debt sustainability analysis of the enhanced HIPC Initiative is built on the flimsiest of foundations" (Sachs, 2002, p. 275).

2. Objectivity of HIPC eligibility criteria

(a) The poverty criterion

While the HIPC Initiative is supposed to be targeted at the world's poorest countries, it defines the poorest countries in terms of the "IDA/PRGF-only" criterion, which is a narrow income-per-capita-determined criterion.[29] There is currently a consensus that a monetary measure of poverty is too simple and narrow to capture the multifaceted nature of poverty. Poverty has been described as "an interlocking web of economic, political, human and sociocultural deprivations, [and] characterised by insecurity, vulnerability and powerlessness" (see UNCTAD, 2002b, which contains a detailed analysis of the multifaceted nature of poverty).

If the Initiative's definition of poverty had embraced its multidimensional nature, the group of countries eligible for HIPC debt relief would have been radically different from the current group. In this connection, table 6, based on data on GNI per capita and UNDP's human poverty index (HPI-1), which takes account of the multifaceted nature of poverty,[30] makes a comparison with the IDA/PRGF-only categorization for all African countries as well as for the non-African HIPCs. It illustrates, for example, that if the HPI-1 index is used, the ratings of all African countries for which there are data (except Mauritius) would fall below that of Bolivia and Guyana, which are eligible for debt relief under the HIPC Initiative.

Political and cost factors may also have played a significant role in defining HIPC eligibility thresholds. Originally, the Initiative was to address the debt problems of low-income countries, but in its final form, its eligibility was limited to "IDA/PRGF-only" countries. This implied that some countries, such as Nigeria, became ineligible for debt relief under the Initiative.[31] Undoubtedly, the cost of providing HIPC debt relief to such countries would have been much higher.

Furthermore, it appears that there have been inconsistencies even in the application of the IDA/PRGF-only criterion. While some IDA/PRGF-only countries (the Comoros, the Gambia, and Malawi) were added to the original list of HIPCs as it became clear that their debt was higher than initially estimated, heavily indebted IDA/PRGF-only countries like the Kyrgyz Republic were not added, as it was argued that transition economies should be treated separately. Similarly, Equatorial Guinea was excluded because its income per capita exceeded the IDA/PRGF income per capita limit. However, Bolivia's enhanced HIPC debt relief was approved in February 2000, even though its per capita income had been above the operational cut-off point since 1997.[32]

(b) Debt sustainability criteria

There is a strongly argued view in the debt literature that the Initiative's debt sustainability criteria are not objective and lack a robust theoretical justification (see especially Gunter, 2003; Hjertholm, 2003; and Sachs, 2002). However, the World Bank's OED Review (Gautam, 2003) did not consider the debt sustainability criteria to be a major problem, as different indicators have their advantages and disadvantages. On the other hand, the Bretton Woods institutions, by proposing a new methodology for assessing debt sustainability, have implicitly accepted the weakness of the enhanced HIPC debt sustainability criteria and the need for some reconsideration and revisions (see for example, IMF and World Bank, 2004b).

The debt sustainability analysis within the context of the HIPC Initiative utilizes two main debt indicators, the NPV debt-to-exports ratio and NPV debt-to-revenue ratio. In addition, four generally available and broadly accepted debt indicators could be used to determine sustainable debt levels of countries:

(a) NPV debt-to-gross national income (GNI) ratio;

(b) Debt service-to-GNI ratio;

(c) Debt service-to-exports ratio; and

(d) Debt service-to-revenue ratio.

The indebtedness of Africa is examined based on these six indicators, the three-year averages (2000–2002) of which are presented in table 7. In accordance with the principles of the HIPC Initiative, debt and debt service is limited to public and publicly guaranteed external debt, although exports of goods and services include exports of factor services, and the three-year averages cover both numerators and denominators in all ratios. First, it is evident from table 7 that these six debt indicators reveal large differences in debt sustainability across countries. Second, the table suggests that Africa's debt problem is much greater than suggested by the official group of African countries eligible for enhanced HIPC debt relief. For example, two HIPCs (Tanzania and Uganda) have lower debt ratios than some African non-HIPCs (Djibouti, Eritrea, Lesotho, Nigeria and Zimbabwe), based on NPV debt-to-GNI ratios, and Cape Verde, Nigeria and Zimbabwe using NPV debt-to-revenue ratios. These conclusions are further strengthened by the review (below) of the appropriateness of the current HIPC debt indicators, i.e. the NPV debt-to-export criterion and the NPV debt-to-revenue ratio; as well as by the discussion on whether domestic debt should be considered when determineing appropriate threshold levels. The other four indicators are discussed in the section on "alternative debt sustainability criteria".

Table 6

HIPCs AND OTHER AFRICAN COUNTRIES: COMPARISONS BASED ON PER CAPITA INCOME, POVERTY (HPI-1) AND IDA-ONLY CATEGORY

	GNI per capita (dollars, 2000–2002 average)	UNDP's Human Poverty Index-1	IDA-only category
African HIPCs:			
Eligible:			
Benin	383	46.4	yes
Burkina Faso	247	58.6	yes
Cameroon	567	35.9	yes
Chad	200	50.3	yes
Dem. Republic of the Congo	93	42.9	yes
Ethiopia	107	56.0	yes
Gambia	307	45.8	yes
Ghana	297	26.4	yes
Guinea	427	n.a.	yes
Guinea-Bissau	143	47.8	yes
Madagascar	247	35.9	yes
Malawi	163	47.0	yes
Mali	233	55.1	yes
Mauritania	330	48.6	yes
Mozambique	203	50.3	yes
Niger	180	61.8	yes
Rwanda	243	44.5	yes
Sao Tome and Principe[1]	293	n.a.	yes
Senegal	487	44.5	yes
Sierra Leone	133	na	yes
Uganda	253	36.6	yes
United Republic of Tanzania	277	36.2	yes
Zambia	330	50.3	yes
Non-eligible:			
Angola	570	n.a.	yes
Kenya	353	37.8	yes
To be decided:			
Burundi	103	46.3	yes
Central African Republic	267	47.8	yes
Comoros	383	31.5	yes
Congo	563	32.0	yes
Côte d'Ivoire	650	45.0	yes
Liberia[1]	137	n.a.	yes
Somalia	n.a.	n.a.	yes
Sudan	350	32.2	yes
Togo	277	38.5	yes

Table 6 (contd.)

	GNI per capita (dollars, 2000–2002 average)	UNDP's Human Poverty Index-1	IDA-only category
Other African countries:			
Algeria	1 653	22.6	no
Botswana	3 073	43.6	no
Cape Verde	1 283	20.1	no
Djibouti	840	34.3	no
Egypt	1 497	30.5	no
Equatorial Guinea[1]	815	n.a.	no
Eritrea	187	41.8	no
Gabon	3 093	n.a.	no
Lesotho	597	47.7	no
Libya[1]	n.a.	15.7	no
Mauritius	3 800	11.1	no
Morocco	1 180	35.2	no
Namibia	1 953	37.8	no
Nigeria	290	34.0	no
Seychelles	7 087	n.a.	no
South Africa	2 740	31.7	no
Swaziland	1 320	n.a.	no
Tunisia	2 043	19.9	no
Zimbabwe[1]	460	52.0	no
Non-African HIPCs:			
Eligible:			
Bolivia	940	14.6	yes[2]
Guyana	860	12.7	yes
Honduras	903	19.9	yes
Lao PDR	300	40.5	yes
Myanmar	0	25.7	yes
Nicaragua	610	24.3	yes
Non-eligible:			
Viet Nam	407	19.9	yes
Yemen	460	41.0	yes

Source: IDA eligibility: World Bank Operational Policies, OP3.10-Annex D (July 2003); GNI per capita: World Bank, *Global Development Finance* and *World Development Indicators, 2004*; Human Poverty Index: UNDP, *Human Development Report 2003*.

[1] GNI per capita based on 2000–2001 average or latest available.
[2] Bolivia formally became a blend country (no more IDA-only) on 1 July 2001.

Table 7

SELECTED DEBT INDICATORS (2000–2002 AVERAGES)[1]

(Percentages)

	NPV debt-to-GNI	Debt service-to-GNI	NPV debt-to-XGS	Debt service-to-XGS	NPV debt-to-revenue	Debt service-to-revenue
African HIPCs:						
Eligible:						
Benin	34	2.5	131	9.5	209	15.2
Burkina Faso	22	1.6	194	14.3	193	14.0
Cameroon	58	4.8	193	15.8	298	24.5
Chad	39	1.6	222	9.3	537	22.2
Dem. Rep. of the Congo[2]	219	6.4	980	29.5	3 455	76.0
Ethiopia	48	2.1	303	13.6	270	11.9
Gambia[3]	67	4.5	97	6.6	431	28.4
Ghana	66	5.5	155	13.2	401	34.8
Guinea	51	4.1	197	15.7	469	37.2
Guinea-Bissau	231	9.6	781	32.8	1 390	58.2
Madagascar	48	2.2	179	8.2	451	20.4
Malawi	77	2.6	273	9.4	416	14.2
Mali	53	3.4	144	9.1	304	19.3
Mauritania	131	8.3	324	20.2	573	33.5
Mozambique	30	2.3	115	8.6	224	17.4
Niger	45	1.4	268	8.2	495	14.6
Rwanda	35	1.3	432	16.4	348	13.2
Sao Tome and Principe	236	10.7	596	26.8	967	43.2
Senegal	51	4.6	150	13.5	281	25.2
Sierra Leone	119	8.1	872	60.4	1 025	69.6
Uganda	19	1.1	108	6.4	175	10.2
United Rep. of Tanzania	16	1.8	102	11.2	148	16.1
Zambia	126	6.2	395	19.6	626	31.4
Non-eligible:						
Angola	133	20.2	121	17.5	218	31.1
Kenya	42	4.5	150	16.0	188	20.1
To be decided:						
Burundi	98	3.2	1'472	48.3	499	16.4
Central African Republic	62	0.9	570	8.7	576	9.6
Comoros	81	1.5	528	9.6	606	10.5
Congo	229	2.7	188	2.2	544	6.2
Côte d'Ivoire	99	7.8	212	16.7	560	44.3
Liberia[2]	477	0.2	1'445	0.5	n.a.	n.a.
Somalia	n.a.	n.a.	n.a.	n.a.	n.a.	n.a.
Sudan[2]	133	0.4	575	1.8	1 027	3.3
Togo	83	2.0	210	5.0	593	14.5

Table 7 (contd.)

	NPV debt-to-GNI	Debt service-to-GNI	NPV debt-to-XGS	Debt service-to-XGS	NPV debt-to-revenue	Debt service-to-revenue
Other african countries:						
Algeria	45	8.5	114	21.8	113	21.6
Botswana	7	1.2	11	1.9	16	2.6
Cape Verde	41	3.0	91	6.6	195	14.2
Djibouti	33	2.1	85	5.4	n.a.	n.a.
Egypt	26	2.0	124	9.4	133	10.2
Equatorial Guinea	52	1.2	6	0.1	64	1.5
Eritrea	31	0.8	158	4.0	132	3.6
Gabon	89	10.2	108	12.3	316	35.9
Lesotho	41	6.3	78	11.9	135	20.8
Libya	n.a.	n.a.	n.a.	n.a.	n.a.	n.a.
Mauritius	37	6.9	58	11.1	199	36.5
Morocco	46	8.6	110	20.7	181	34.2
Namibia	n.a.	n.a.	n.a.	n.a.	n.a.	n.a.
Nigeria	84	5.3	144	8.9	163	10.2
Seychelles	39	2.3	43	2.5	97	5.8
South Africa	20	3.5	64	11.4	87	15.5
Swaziland	22	2.0	24	2.2	90	8.0
Tunisia	57	7.9	110	15.5	219	30.0
Zimbabwe	62	3.7	184	10.2	184	10.6
Non-African HIPCs:						
Eligible:						
Bolivia	26	6.8	121	32.0	114	30.0
Guyana	134	9.8	123	9.0	388	28.3
Honduras	54	6.3	105	12.2	283	32.8
Lao PDR	83	2.7	272	8.7	523	16.7
Myanmar[4]	0.9	0.02	157	3.6	19	0.4
Nicaragua	130	8.6	304	20.0	618	40.9
Non-eligible:						
Viet Nam	34	3.8	60	6.7	163	18.1
Yemen	45	2.8	71	4.3	111	6.7

Source: Calculated based on various World Bank databases; see note 1 for further details.

[1] Subject to availability, averages have been calculated based on individual year ratios, whereby the latest availalbe data have been used to calculate each year's ratio before taking the average over the three years. All debt data are based on total external debt and actual total debt service paid as reported in the World Bank's Global Development Finance databases.

The net present value (NPV) debt data for year 2000 have been estimated based on country-specific ratios of nominal debt to NPV debt of year 2001. GNI, export and revenue data are taken from various World Bank databases, whereby exports of goods and services include factor payments, and government revenues exclude grants.

[2] Substantial arrears (which are considered to be due) push the NPV debt ratios up, while debt service paid is far below what is due and thus pushes the debt service ratios down.

[3] Excluding worker's remittances and re-exports, Gambia's NPV debt-to-export ratio increases to over 200%.

[4] Due to lack of data on GNI, the GDP data, calculated based on the official exchange rate, was used, which deflates the NPV and debt service to GNI indicators.

(i) NPV debt-to-export ratio criterion

The debt-to-export ratio criterion has been used for mostly middle-income Latin American countries in the aftermath of the 1982 debt crisis. However, the situation in Latin America then was different from that of today's HIPCs. First, a substantial part of Latin American debt was commercial bank debt; and second, exchange rate devaluations following the outbreak of the 1982 debt crisis led to substantial trade surpluses with which debt service payments were financed. In contrast to Latin America, with the exception of four HIPCs (Bolivia, Côte d'Ivoire, Honduras and Mozambique), nearly all of the HIPCs' external debt is public or publicly guaranteed. Furthermore, substantial devaluations cannot be the solution for the debt problems of HIPC economies because most HIPC economies depend heavily on ODA and imports, and there are very limited options for many HIPCs to increase exports under current global realities because of their dependence on non-fuel primary commodity exports (see UNCTAD, 2003). In addition, in a few cases, exports of African HIPCs include a large proportion of re-exports, but the HIPC framework has not been consistent in either including or excluding re-exports in the calculation of the debt-to-export criterion. This could lead to significant distortions in debt ratios and problems of comparability of such ratios between different HIPCs.

(ii) NPV debt-to-revenue ratio

There appears to be no theoretical foundation for the required thresholds for the fiscal window. As Martin (2002, p. 3) points out, the NPV debt-to-revenue ratio, which is also commonly referred to as the Côte d'Ivoire criterion, "was set at a level just low enough to include one country in the HIPC group... but was accompanied by empirically unjustified sub-criteria which exclude many other HIPCs [low-income countries]." While it can be argued that the thresholds are justified to provide some incentives for countries to increase their exports-to-GDP and revenue-to-GDP ratios, it should be noted that ratios below the thresholds usually reflect structural problems, that are unlikely to be overcome in the short-term. Furthermore, given that the eligible countries are required to have undergone three years of "successful" economic reforms supported by the IMF and the World Bank before reaching their decision point, it is difficult to argue that HIPC eligibility should be based on this sort of incentive and/or that without these thresholds, the HIPC Initiative would reward countries with weak economic policies. This is particularly so because, in some cases, increases in export-to-GDP and revenue-to-GDP ratios have also been used as triggers (or conditionalities) for reaching the completion point.

Table 8 shows that without HIPC debt relief, 17 of the 27 enhanced decision point HIPCs would have had an NPV debt-to-revenue ratio of more than 250 per cent.[33] Yet 11 of these 17 HIPCs did not qualify for debt relief under the fiscal window due to the threshold requirements. While these 11 fiscally unsustainable HIPCs still qualified for HIPC debt relief under the export criterion, the debt relief provided under the export criterion has been below what would be needed to obtain an NPV debt-to-government revenue ratio of a maximum of 250 per cent for three of them (Democratic Republic of Congo, the Gambia, and Guinea).

Furthermore, table 9 shows that 19 of the 27 HIPCs that reached the enhanced decision point by the end of 2003 are expected to spend at least 10 per cent of government revenues on servicing public external debt for at least two years during the period 2003-2005. The Democratic Republic of Congo, the Gambia, Guinea, Sierra Leone, Sao Tome and Principe, and Zambia were expected to devote more than 20 per cent of government revenues to servicing their public external debt in at least one of the three years during the period in question.

Within the group of 27 HIPCs, there is only one country (Burkina Faso) that is expected to spend an average of slightly less than 5 per cent of government government revenues to service its public external debt during 2003-2005.

Furthermore, as discussed below, given that the HIPC Initiative excludes domestic public debt, this indicator loses some of its usefulness, especially as there are considerable differences in the amounts of domestic public debt across HIPCs.

(iii) Domestic debt

In order for the HIPC Initiative to provide for overall debt sustainability of the poorest countries as a precondition for achieving sustainable growth and development, a country's domestic public debt (and especially the amount of debt service on public domestic debt) should be included in the debt sustainability analysis. Indeed, servicing domestic debt adds as much, if not more, to a Government's fiscal burden as servicing external debt. In the late 1990s, the high cost of domestic debts in many SSA countries led to an increase in domestic debt service payments (exceeding external debt service payments in several cases) in total government expenditures, thereby worsening the

Table 8

NPV DEBT-TO-REVENUE RATIOS, WITH AND WITHOUT HIPC DEBT RELIEF

	NPV debt-to-revenue ratio for 2003 (in per cent)	
	Without HIPC debt relief	*With HIPC debt relief*
Benin	163	113
Bolivia	161	113
Burkina Faso	137	69
Cameroon	199	145
Chad	258	181
Dem. Rep. of the Congo	1 306	261
Ethiopia	191	101
Gambia	424	310
Ghana	413	182
Guinea	445	303
Guinea-Bissau	1 152	173
Guyana	333	200
Honduras	225	185
Madagascar	395	237
Malawi	413	231
Mali	203	144
Mauritania	382	191
Mozambique	192	141
Nicaragua	665	186
Niger	349	160
Rwanda	284	82
Sao Tome and Principe	851	145
Senegal	233	189
Sierra Leone	585	117
Uganda	220	139
United Republic of Tanzania	312	144
Zambia	576	213

Source: Calculations based on IMF and World Bank (2003a), and the HIPC Status Table.

Table 9

PROJECTIONS ON PUBLIC EXTERNAL DEBT SERVICE-TO-GOVERNMENT REVENUES,
2003–2005

(Percentages)

	2003	2004	2005
Benin	5.9	5.3	5.3
Bolivia	15.8	15.2	16.2
Burkina Faso	5.3	4.7	4.3
Cameroon	12.3	12.0	11.2
Chad	18.3	11.3	10.0
Dem. Rep. of the Congo	24.8	28.6	24.6
Ethiopia	6.2	6.0	5.3
Gambia	26.5	19.8	20.5
Ghana	17.3	10.0	7.9
Guinea	23.3	19.5	15.4
Guinea-Bissau	12.0	13.6	7.5
Guyana	18.8	14.0	12.9
Honduras	17.1	13.4	12.6
Madagascar	10.4	12.6	11.2
Malawi	18.9	9.6	11.7
Mali	8.4	8.1	7.7
Mauritania	16.6	17.7	17.0
Mozambique	8.0	7.6	7.5
Nicaragua	17.3	12.8	13.3
Niger	9.4	9.7	9.0
Rwanda	5.8	6.4	5.6
Sao Tome and Principe	23.3	10.7	4.5
Senegal	13.3	11.8	10.7
Sierra Leone	12.8	28.0	13.7
Uganda	9.3	9.7	9.4
United Rep. of Tanzania	8.3	9.5	10.0
Zambia	27.2	31.3	27.5
Weighted average	**13.4**	**12.5**	**11.7**

Source: IMF and World Bank (2003a), appendix table 3.

budget deficit. For example, in Kenya's 1999/2000 budget, funds allocated to servicing domestic debt were more than double those allocated to servicing external debt, which was about three times the stock of domestic debt (Rwegasira and Mwega, 2003, pp. 264–265).

There is a close linkage between accumulation of external debt and domestic debt, as economic agents borrow to fill the private savings-investment gap, the fiscal gap and/or the foreign-exchange gap (Ibid, p. 267). In their alternative framework for debt sustainability, Fedelino and Kudina (2003, p. 6) take into account external and domestic liabilities because, first, while external debt may be sustainable, the total stock of debt may not be when domestic debt is also included in total debt stocks, and second, to the extent that HIPCs do not have access to international capital markets and rely on ODA flows, domestic financing may become a significant source of funds with important macroeconomic and debt sustainability implications. Thus, neglecting domestic debt might underestimate the required magnitude of the fiscal effort to be made and/or external assistance needed by HIPCs in the post-completion point period to reach real debt sustainability.

Many arguments have been advanced against the inclusion of public domestic debt. For instance, public domestic debt is small, data are rare and can be manipulated, and there are definitional problems regarding what exactly constitutes "public domestic debt". In addition, the World Bank has argued that actions to control or reduce public domestic debt fall under the purview of the IMF's Poverty Reduction and Growth Facility (PRGF) within the context of overall domestic fiscal management. The main reason given for this is the lack of empirical thresholds for assessing the appropriate level of public domestic debt, hence monitoring and interpreting it becomes difficult (Gautam, 2003). In the opinion of both the IMF and the World Bank, the implications of domestic debt for an appropriate forward-looking financial strategy must be judged on a case-by-case basis (IMF and World Bank, 2004b).

The IMF has access to data on domestic debt of all eligible HIPCs as part of the HIPC eligibility requirement. Moreover, the sustained implementation of integrated poverty reduction and economic reform programmes for at least three years includes the collection and monitoring of data on debt service payments on domestic public debt. Table 10 provides estimates of the size and share of public domestic debt for some African countries based on recently published IMF Staff Reports. Clearly, there are considerable differences across

Table 10

DOMESTIC PUBLIC DEBT OF AFRICAN HIPCS:

DEBT STOCK AND INTEREST PAYMENTS, 2000–2002 AVERAGE

	Interest payments due on domestic public debt		Stock of domestic public debt	
	Value in $ millions	*In % of total interest payments*	*Value in $ millions*	*In % of total public debt*
HIPC eligible:				
Benin	2.2	10.5	43.8	2.5
Burkina Faso	6.9	29.3	138.5	8.5
Cameroon	32.4	10.5	648.7	7.1
Chad	2.3	14.9	45.8	3.8
Dem. Rep. of the Congo	8.4	3.0	167.4	1.5
Ethiopia	80.0	54.1	1 600.6	21.3
Gambia	14.5	76.5	289.0	36.0
Ghana	288.6	74.1	5 772.1	46.5
Guinea[1]	39.1	42.4	781.3	18.9
Guinea-Bissau	0.6	3.4	11.2	1.5
Madagascar	36.4	39.5	728.9	14.0
Malawi	63.4	71.0	1 268.5	31.6
Mali	2.1	9.0	42.3	1.4
Mauritania	5.2	17.5	104.6	4.2
Mozambique[1]	5.7	27.4	114.9	3.0
Niger	2.2	7.0	44.9	2.7
Rwanda[1]	5.1	32.2	101.7	7.1
Sao Tome and Principe	0.1	2.8	2.3	0.7
Senegal	7.7	15.1	153.6	4.1
Sierra Leone	23.7	56.7	474.8	26.4
Uganda	38.4	50.1	767.1	16.9
United Rep. of Tanzania	81.2	58.2	1 623.9	18.7
Zambia	68.3	58.6	1 366.4	19.4
Non-HIPC eligible:				
Angola	0.0	0.0	0.0	0.0
Kenya	271.5	72.5	5 430.2	48.3
HIPC eligibility to be determined:				
Burundi	9.8	46.3	196.1	14.8
Central African Republic	3.1	19.8	61.3	6.3
Comoros	0.1	5.9	2.6	1.0
Congo	14.9	6.4	298.6	5.8
Côte d'Ivoire	35.5	9.1	710.8	6.3
Liberia	n.a.	n.a.	n.a.	n.a.
Somalia	n.a.	n.a.	n.a.	n.a.
Sudan	13.5	10.1	269.6	1.7
Togo	3.4	12.4	68.8	4.5

Sources: Calculations based on interest payments on domestic and external public debt as reported in country-specific IMF Staff Reports and World Bank databases; stocks of domestic public debt are estimates based on interest payments on public domestic debt, assuming that the average interest rate on domestic public debt is 5 per cent.

[1] Data based on period 1999–2001.

African HIPCs in the amounts and shares of domestic public debt and debt service. The use of an average based on actual historical data for the calculation of HIPC debt relief, as is the case for any determinant of debt relief, would reduce the incentives to manipulate domestic debt data for the purpose of receiving more HIPC debt relief.

Even though domestic debt is small compared to external debt, its influence on fiscal debt sustainability could be great. As shown in table 10, between 2000 and 2002, for 10 of the 23 African HIPCs at the decision or completion point, the stock of domestic public debt as a proportion of total public debt was quite high, ranging from about 17 per cent (Tanzania) to 47 per cent for Ghana and 48 per cent for Kenya, a country whose external debt is deemed sustainable under the HIPC Initiative. The fiscal burden of public domestic debt appears even greater if interest payments are taken into consideration. A third of total interest payments by 12 of the 23 African HIPCs is on public domestic debt. Of all interest payments by the Gambia, for example, 77 per cent is on domestic debt. The comparable figure for Kenya is 73 per cent. Thus, public domestic debt could prove a bottleneck for many low-income countries in achieving total debt sustainability, even if it were possible to reduce their external debt to sustainable levels within the context of the Initiative.

Furthermore, the trends in macroeconomic indicators in a large number of African countries are influenced by the high domestic interest rates and the short maturity periods on domestic instruments. Public domestic debt in these countries has maturity periods of usually less than two years due to the under-developed domestic capital markets, and until recently interest rates were generally very high in many African countries. In a survey by the IMF on the maturity of domestic debt for selected African countries (of which seven are HIPCs) and emerging-market countries, the average maturity of debt instruments for the African countries was less than one year (231 days), while that for a select group of developed and emerging markets was about five years (1,945 days).[34] In the survey, domestic debt markets in HIPCs appeared to have the shortest maturity structure of about six months (177 days) (IMF, 1999). This dominance of short-term paper in African securities markets increases rollover and market risks, especially in countries with large outstanding domestic debt stocks.

As shown in an earlier UNCTAD study, in many developing countries interest payments on domestic debt absorb large and increasing proportions of the national budget, and high interest rates raise interest payments on government debt at the expense of social spending and distort income distribution (UNCTAD, 2002a). Under such circumstances, "it is impossible to ensure adequate resources for poverty reduction spending unless we analyse and resolve the domestic debt problem" (Debt Relief International, 2003). It is important to stress that the inclusion of public domestic debt in HIPC debt sustainability analyses does not necessarily imply the inclusion of public domestic debt in the determination of the amount of overall HIPC debt relief.

3. Examples of alternative debt sustainability criteria

The typical definition of debt sustainability for analytical purposes is based on the determination as to whether a country can meet its current and future debt service obligations in full, without recourse to debt relief, rescheduling or accumulation of arrears. This is usually a difficult determination to make, however, as a debt sustainability analysis is by definition forward-looking and takes into account many variables the values of which cannot be predicted with much certainty. Most of the literature on debt sustainability analyses debt dynamics over an infinite horizon and then derives some kind of solvency conditions according to which debt sustainability can be determined.

However, given the practical limitations of such infinite horizon solvency conditions, practitioners have suggested more practical debt sustainability indicators, whereby it is useful to distinguish between (i) nominal stock-of-debt indicators, (ii) NPV debt indicators,[35] and (iii) debt service indicators. Nominal stock-of-debt indicators have been used widely for industrialized country applications.[36] NPV debt indicators are more appropriate for developing countries, as they make it possible to take into account differences in concessionality levels. Debt service indicators are most useful for assessing short-term debt sustainability and vulnerability.[37]

To allow for comparisons across countries, each indicator is usually expressed in terms of another macroeconomic variable, and the three most common macroeconomic variables used as denominators for a debt or debt service ratio are (i) income, (ii) exports, and (iii) government revenues. There obviously exist a variety of options for defining each of these macroeconomic variables. For example, the most often used income categories are gross domestic product (GDP), gross national product (GNP), gross domestic income (GDI) or gross national income (GNI).[38] Exports may include workers' remittances and re-exports. They could also be based on current-year values or be averaged over some time period. The HIPC framework excludes workers' remittances, while it has been inconsistent with regard to the inclusion or exclusion of re-exports.[39] The inclusion or exclusion of re-exports could lead to significant distortions in debt-to-export ratios. In the case of the Gambia, for example, including re-exports resulted in a ratio of about 127 per cent, but excluding them gave an NPV debt-to-export ratio of 216 per cent and thus made the Gambia eligible for enhanced HIPC debt relief.

To reduce the impact of fluctuations in yearly data, especially in respect of the denominator of a debt ratio, it is usually preferred to use multi-year averages. The HIPC Initiative uses three-year backward-looking averages for exports and revenues in calculating its NPV debt-to-export and NPV debt-to-revenue ratios. Finally, given that each indicator has its limitations, it is also useful to look at more than one or two debt indicators to determine a country's debt sustainability.

The World Bank's *Global Development Finance* (GDF) (formerly, *World Debt Tables*; see http://www.worldbank.org/prospects/gdf2003/) classifies external indebtedness on the basis of two ratios, namely the ratio of the NPV of total external debt to the three-year backward-looking average of GNI, and the ratio of the NPV of total external debt to the three-year backward-looking average of exports of goods and services (including workers' remittances and re-exports). If either ratio exceeds a critical value — 80 per cent for the NPV debt-to-GNI ratio and 220 per cent for the NPV debt-to-exports ratio — the country is classified as severely indebted. If the critical value is not exceeded but either ratio is three-fifths or more of the critical value (that is, 48 per cent for the NPV debt-to-GNI ratio and 132 per cent for the NPV debt-to-exports ratio), the country is classified as moderately indebted. If both ratios are less than three-fifths of the critical value, the country is classified as less indebted.

Looking specifically at the debt indicators of the HIPC framework, a report by a group of independent reviewers stressed that "the ratios of debt and debt service to exports (...) are hard to justify on theoretical grounds" and that "at the very least, indicators relative to GDP should be taken as seriously as indicators relative to exports."[40] Birdsall and Williamson (2002) have considered the NPV debt-to-GNP ratio as a useful indicator. While completely ignored in the HIPC framework, an NPV debt-to-income ratio is a good overall indicator of a country's indebtedness. It also has the advantages of being less volatile than the NPV debt-to-exports indicator and more easily available than the NPV debt-to-government revenue indicator.

It is also important to keep the two main purposes of the debt sustainability analysis in mind — determining the sustainability of a country's external debt, and estimating the fiscal sustainability of a country's public debt. When analysing a country's external debt sustainability, the debt category should usually include all external debt, whether it is public or private. If analysing a country's fiscal sustainability, the debt category should usually include all public debt, both foreign and domestic. Using a specific debt variable usually also has implications for the use of a macroeconomic denominator for a debt and a debt service ratio. For example, it is inappropriate to use the export denominator if analysing a country's total (foreign and domestic) fiscal debt sustainability. Similarly, the use of the revenue denominator is not appropriate if analysing a country's total (public and private) foreign debt sustainability. External debt sustainability is not sufficient for fiscal sustainability and vice versa.

In general, while it is not possible to provide a definitive answer on which debt indicator is the most useful, there is some agreement that:

   (i) NPV debt and debt service to income (defined as either GDP, GNP, GDI, or GNI) ratios are useful comprehensive indicators;

  (ii) NPV total external debt and NPV debt service to export ratios are useful indicators for external debt sustainability analyses; and

 (iii) NPV total public debt and NPV debt service to government revenue ratios are useful indicators for fiscal debt sustainability analyses.

Except in cases where arbitrary thresholds are satisfied, the Initiative ignores issues related to fiscal sustainability, and even in cases where the thresholds for the fiscal window are satisfied, as indicated earlier the HIPC framework's NPV public external debt-to-revenue ratio excludes domestic public debt. However, a major issue in very poor African countries, which are vulnerable to unremitting external shocks, is the extent to which the NPV of debt-to-export criterion, for example, realistically reflects sustainable debt levels, in particular considering that debt sustainability analysis is highly probabilistic and forward-looking.

4. Non-HIPC debt-distressed African countries

As indicated earlier, table 7 provides the data for six broadly available and broadly accepted debt indicators averaged over three years (2000–2002) for all African countries. For comparison purposes, data are also included for the non-African HIPCs. While the data always include private external debt, they always exclude (due to data constraints and subsequent comparability reasons) all domestic debt. Table 7 shows that a number of non-HIPC African countries have, based on at least two debt indicators, relative high debt levels and can thus be considered to be debt-distressed. Beyond the African HIPCs the debts of which are considered to be sustainable under the HIPC framework, such as Angola and Kenya, the most obvious case of a non-HIPC debt-distressed African country is Nigeria (see boxes 1 and 2).

Box 1

Kenya: HIPC with "sustainable" debt

In 1970, Kenya's total external debt was less than $500 million. Ten years later it stood at $3.4 billion. It continued to grow sharply during the 1980s and the early 1990s, reaching a maximum of $7.4 billion in 1995. It then decreased slowly to about $6 billion in 2001, of which about $5 billion was public and publicly guaranteed (see World Bank, 2002).

In addition to a large external debt, Kenya had about $2.5 billion (KSH 222 billion) of domestic public debt as of December 2001.[41] Kenya's domestic public debt has increased sharply during the last few years, reflecting the recent deterioration of the country's fiscal balance, from a surplus of 1 per cent of GDP in 1999 to a deficit of 2.7 per cent of GDP in 2002, largely due to a fall in revenues, a contraction in donor inflows, a decline in the productivity of public outlays, and a rise in public debt service payments. Given that the deficit has — due to lack of external financing — been financed increasingly through domestic borrowing, the stock of domestic debt increased to nearly 30 per cent of GDP in November 2002.

According to the HIPC framework, Kenya is not eligible for HIPC debt relief as its debt is considered to be sustainable. Yet Were (2001) shows that, even ignoring domestic debt, the country's external debt has had a negative impact on its economic growth. The HIPC framework neglects not only Kenya's large domestic debt but also the financing required to eradicate or at least to significantly reduce the country's extreme poverty, which is the declared goal of Kenya's new Government. Given that 62 per cent of Kenya's population (of about 30 million) live on less than $2 a day, and that more than one quarter lives below $1 a day, debt relief could go

Box 1 (contd.)

a long way towards reducing Kenya's extreme poverty. For example, Nafula (2002) demonstrates that debt relief would help the country to achieve universal primary education.

Finally, as Birdsall and Williamson (2002, pp. 131–2) illustrate in more detail, the argument for odious debt is strong in the case of Kenya, as a corrupt ruling elite expropriated billions of dollars in waste and in amassing personal fortunes, partly with the knowledge and support of Kenya's creditors.

Box 2

NIGERIA: NON-HIPC DEBT-DISTRESSED AFRICAN COUNTRY

Nigeria is one of the poorest countries in the world. With a GNI per capita of $290, Nigeria ranks far below the average HIPC. According to UNDP's human poverty index, the country, with an index of 34.0, is also poorer than 10 eligible HIPCs. Yet the IMF and the World Bank have not classified Nigeria as an IDA/PRGF-only country, as it is argued that Nigeria does not, due to its large oil resources, rely on IDA/PRGF resources. Though it is formally a "blend country", which is defined as a country that is eligible for IDA resources on the basis of per capita income but has limited creditworthiness to borrow from the International Bank for Reconstruction and Development (IBRD, the World Bank's non-concessional window), Nigeria is not supposed to borrow on other than highly concessional terms.[42]

It is by now widely recognized that natural resources do not always bring the expected benefits of growth and development. Indeed in some of the poorest countries, resources have been a curse, as they tend to invite corruption and induce civil conflicts that are difficult to tackle through weak governance structures and in countries with low rates of literacy.[43] Indeed, Nigeria's oil revenues have not been sufficient to generate enough income for growth and poverty reduction. As Sala-i-Martin and Subramanian (2003) show, Nigeria's poverty rate (measured by the share of the population subsisting on less than a $1 a day) increased from about 36 per cent in 1970 to about 70 per cent in 2000.

With an average NPV debt-to-export ratio of 163 per cent and an average NPV debt-to-gross national income (GNI) ratio of 82 per cent, it is also clear that Nigeria is severely indebted, and it is classified as such by the World Bank's *Global Development Finance*. Furthermore, owing to its status as a relatively open economy due to high oil exports, the country's external debt indicators (like the NPV debt-to-export ratio) do not adequately reflect the fiscal burden of its external debt. Considering that data on Nigeria's government revenues are not publicly available, some insights could be gained into Nigeria's debt distress by looking at its debt service-to-GNI ratio. With an average of 4.9 per cent during the period 1999–2001, the country's debt service-to-GNI ratio is higher than that of at least half of all the eligible HIPCs.

Chapter III

How sustainable is African HIPCs' debt after debt relief?

1. Post-HIPC debt sustainability

The debt overhang literature[44] does not provide conclusive answers or evidence as to what sustainable debt levels are. A recent IMF Working Paper supports the claim that, on the basis of current fiscal policies, debt levels will remain unsustainable in many African HIPCs even after they graduate from the HIPC Initiative (Fedelino and Kudina, 2003). Another recent study by Kraay and Nehru (2003), corroborated by the IMF staff's empirical analysis (see IMF and World Bank, 2004b), finds strong evidence that institutions and policies, as well as external shocks, are important in determining the levels of debt at which countries experience distress. As discussed in the previous chapter, the assessment of debt sustainability is, by its nature, a forward-looking concept and inherently probabilistic.

A Report of the United States General Accounting Office (GAO, 2004) highlights the overly optimistic growth assumptions of HIPC debt sustainability analysis. The report shows that, on the basis of the IMF's and the World Bank's projected growth rates, the average probability of achieving debt sustainability in 2020 was 83.9 per cent for the 27 HIPCs that had reached their enhanced decision point by the end of 2003. If based on historical growth rates, the average probability drops to 45.1 per cent. Limiting the comparison to the 23 African HIPCs that had reached their enhanced decision points by the end of 2003, the probability would be of 82.5 per cent if using the IMF's and the World Bank's growth rates, but only 41.0 per cent if using these countries' historical growth rates (see details in table 11). Serious concerns have thus arisen as to the appropriateness of the basis on which the amount of debt relief is determined within the HIPC framework.

Table 11

LIKELIHOOD OF ACHIEVING DEBT SUSTAINABILITY UNDER DIFFERENT SCENARIOS IN 2020
(Percentages)

	Based on World Bank/ IMF growth rates	Based on historical rates
Benin	89.3	42.3
Bolivia	75.7	11.0
Burkina Faso	76.0	1.7
Cameroon	95.9	63.2
Chad	62.3	51.3
Congo	84.4	1.5
Ethiopia	93.1	37.3
Gambia	91.7	94.2
Ghana	89.4	81.0
Guinea	97.2	37.6
Guinea-Bissau	70.0	65.1
Guyana	97.7	93.2
Honduras	99.5	98.7
Madagascar	99.0	86.7
Malawi	72.3	44.0
Mali	75.4	59.9
Mauritania	98.3	25.3
Mozambique	97.8	77.3
Nicaragua	95.7	72.3
Niger	65.9	2.7
Rwanda	57.3	10.0
Sao Tome and Principe	66.5	12.4
Senegal	98.7	78.9
Serra Leone	81.3	1.5
Uganda	67.4	28.3
United Republic of Tanzania	83.2	35.9
Zambia	85.3	5.4
Average (All 27 countries)	**83.9**	**45.1**
Average (All 23 African countries)	**82.5**	**41.0**

Source: Adapted from GAO (2004).

(a) HIPC methodology to determine the amount of debt relief

Within the enhanced HIPC Initiative, the amount of HIPC debt relief is determined at the decision point, based on the latest available debt sustainability analysis (DSA), which is undertaken usually one year before the decision point.[45] The staff of the IMF and the World Bank, together with officials of the debtor country, prepare the DSA, which gives the amount of debt relief necessary to achieve the appropriate NPV debt-to-export ratio at the decision point. The DSA also makes projections on the future evolution of a HIPC's debt.

While some creditors may provide interim assistance (which counts towards their share of future debt relief), debt relief is usually not due until a HIPC has reached its completion point. Most multilateral financial institutions have usually provided some interim assistance, while the Paris Club usually provides some debt reschedulings. The provision of interim assistance may be interrupted for HIPCs that go off-track with the IMF's programme. Additional debt relief, or "topping-up", beyond what was agreed at the decision point, may be provided at the completion point, in line with the operational framework of the enhanced HIPC Initiative endorsed in September 2001 by the Boards of the IMF and the World Bank. This additional relief is provided only in exceptional circumstances, i.e. in the event of a fundamental change in a country's economic circumstances at the completion point due to exogenous developments.

As of the end of April 2004, HIPC debt relief had been topped up for Burkina Faso, Ethiopia and Niger. Five completion point HIPCs, namely Bolivia, Mauritania, Mozambique, Tanzania, and Uganda, did not have any topping up because they had reached their completion point before the topping up policy was implemented. Three other countries, namely Benin, Mali and Nicaragua, did not meet the conditions for it.

Despite the general consensus that the use of over-optimistic growth rates have led to misleading conclusions regarding HIPCs' debt sustainability, it can be seen from the PRSPs Progress Report (IMF and World Bank, 2003c) that highly optimistic growth rates have continued to be used for some HIPCs' government revenues and to a lesser degree also for some of their exports. With the data provided in table 3 of the appendix to the HIPC Initiative — Status of

Implementation report (IMF and World Bank, 2003a), growth rates of government revenues and exports can be extrapolated for 2004 and 2005 (see tables 12a and 12b below).

While there are a few cases of negative annual growth rates of government revenues from 2003 to 2004 (Sierra Leone (-19.4 per cent); the Gambia (-12.8 per cent); and Guinea-Bissau (-3.1 per cent)), annual growth rates are in 22 cases higher than 10 per cent and in seven cases even higher than 20 per cent. Very high growth rates for revenues between 2003 and 2004 are obtained for Chad (77.3 per cent), the Democratic Republic of Congo (27.6 per cent) and Sao Tome and Principe (42.9 per cent). Similarly, very high growth rates for revenues between 2004 and 2005 have been obtained for the Democratic Republic of Congo (35 per cent), Sao Tome and Principe (24.6 per cent) and Sierra Leone (69 per cent).

Excluding Chad's 2004 outlier of a 329 per cent growth rate for exports, the growth assumptions for the 27 HIPCs' exports are slightly less optimistic than the growth rates for government revenues. There are also a few negative annual growth rates for exports, yet the weighted average of the 27 HIPCs' annual export growth rate remains above seven per cent. More country-specific details reveal that in 11 cases annual export growth rates are higher than 10 per cent and in three cases they are even higher than 20 per cent: Mozambique (44.1 per cent in 2004) and Sierra Leone (25.5 per cent and 22.0 per cent in 2004 and 2005 respectively).

While more moderate economic growth assumptions have relatively small implications for short-run debt ratios, even small differences in the growth assumptions of exports and government revenues have considerable long-term implications that can easily result in highly unsustainable debt situations. Optimistic growth rates affect the HIPC framework's debt sustainability in two ways. First, they affect the debt ratio's denominator, and second, they usually also imply an underestimation of a country's future financing needs. Overestimations of the denominator of a debt ratio and underestimations in the debt ratio numerator would then result in highly unrealistic long-term debt ratios. As the GAO Report (2000, p. 15) pointed out, if Tanzania's exports grow at an annual rate of 6.5 per cent (instead of the 9 per cent projected by the IMF and the World Bank), Tanzania's debt-to-export ratio could be more than twice what the IMF's and the World Bank's forecast shows for the projection period.

Table 12a
Calculations of implicit growth rates for government revenues, 2003–2005

	Projected debt service on public external debt (Millions of dollars) (1)			Debt service-to-government revenues (Per cent) (2)			Projected government revenues, excl. grants (Millions of dollars) (3) = (1)/(2)			Resulting implicit growth rate of government revenues (Per cent)	
	2003	2004	2005	2003	2004	2005	2003	2004	2005	2004	2005
Benin	30.9	30.3	33.5	5.9	5.3	5.3	523.7	571.7	632.1	9.2	10.6
Bolivia	279.3	294.2	327.3	15.8	15.2	16.2	1 767.7	1 935.5	2 020.4	9.5	4.4
Burkina Faso	25.5	26.5	27.3	5.3	4.7	4.3	481.1	563.8	634.9	17.2	12.6
Cameroon	288.5	295.5	288.8	12.3	12.0	11.2	2 345.5	2 462.5	2 578.6	5.0	4.7
Chad	40.2	44.0	46.7	18.3	11.3	10.0	219.7	389.4	467.0	77.3	19.9
Dem. Rep. of the Congo	149.8	220.5	256.0	24.8	28.6	24.6	604.0	771.0	1 040.7	27.6	35.0
Ethiopia	88.0	89.0	88.0	6.2	6.0	5.3	1 419.4	1 483.3	1 660.4	4.5	11.9
Gambia	15.5	10.1	11.0	26.5	19.8	20.5	58.5	51.0	53.7	-12.8	5.2
Ghana	163.5	103.6	111.6	17.3	10.0	7.9	945.1	1 036.0	1 412.7	9.6	36.4
Guinea	89.2	78.9	68.5	23.3	19.5	15.4	382.8	404.6	444.8	5.7	9.9
Guinea-Bissau	5.1	5.6	3.6	12.0	13.6	7.5	42.5	41.2	48.0	-3.1	16.6
Guyana	46.5	37.9	36.2	18.8	14.0	12.9	247.3	270.7	280.6	9.5	3.7
Honduras	234.4	197.6	197.9	17.1	13.4	12.6	1 370.8	1 474.6	1 570.6	7.6	6.5
Madagascar	53.6	72.5	72.7	10.4	12.6	11.2	515.4	575.4	649.1	11.6	12.8
Malawi	66.9	38.9	50.6	18.9	9.6	11.7	354.0	405.2	432.5	14.5	6.7
Mali	59.5	63.0	66.1	8.4	8.1	7.7	708.3	777.8	858.4	9.8	10.4
Mauritania	54.1	60.0	60.8	16.6	17.7	17.0	325.9	339.0	357.6	4.0	5.5
Mozambique	47.1	50.9	57.3	8.0	7.6	7.5	588.8	669.7	764.0	13.8	14.1
Nicaragua	118.1	95.3	105.1	17.3	12.8	13.3	682.7	744.5	790.2	9.1	6.1
Niger	26.0	28.8	29.0	9.4	9.7	9.0	276.6	296.9	322.2	7.3	8.5
Rwanda	13.0	15.5	14.7	5.8	6.4	5.6	224.1	242.2	262.5	8.1	8.4
Sao Tome and Principe	3.2	2.1	1.1	23.3	10.7	4.5	13.7	19.6	24.4	42.9	24.6
Senegal	146.4	141.4	138.7	13.3	11.8	10.7	1 100.8	1 198.3	1 296.3	8.9	8.2
Sierra Leone	16.4	28.9	23.9	12.8	28.0	13.7	128.1	103.2	174.5	-19.4	69.0
Uganda	75.5	85.5	91.5	9.3	9.7	9.4	811.8	886.0	978.6	9.1	10.5
United Rep. of Tanzania	99.8	128.6	148.4	8.3	9.5	10.0	1 202.4	1 353.7	1 484.0	12.6	9.6
Zambia	187.2	222.5	210.4	27.2	31.3	27.5	688.2	710.9	765.1	3.3	7.6
Sum/weighted average	**2 423.2**	**2 467.6**	**2 566.7**	**13.4**	**12.5**	**11.7**	**18 029.0**	**19 777.8**	**22 003.8**	**9.7**	**11.3**

Source: Data for debt service and debt service-to-government revenues are based on IMF and   World Bank (2003a); the erroneous data for Uganda have been corrected with data provided in the 2002 Uganda DSA Update.

Table 12b
CALCULATIONS OF IMPLICIT GROWTH RATES FOR EXPORTS, 2003–2005

	Projected debt service on public external debt (Millions of dollars)			Debt service-to-exports (Per cent)			Projected exports (Millions of dollars)			Resulting implicit growth rate of exports (Per cent)	
	2003	2004	2005	2003	2004	2005	2003	2004	2005	2004	2005
	(1)			(2)			(3) = (1) / (2)				
Benin	30.9	30.3	33.5	6.8	6.0	6.0	454.4	505.0	558.3	11.1	10.6
Bolivia	279.3	294.2	327.3	16.7	16.1	16.7	1 672.5	1 827.3	1 959.9	9.3	7.3
Burkina Faso	25.5	26.5	27.3	8.6	8.3	8.0	296.5	319.3	341.3	7.7	6.9
Cameroon	288.5	295.5	288.8	9.8	10.5	10.4	2 943.9	2 814.3	2 776.9	-4.4	-1.3
Chad	40.2	44.0	46.7	9.8	2.5	2.3	410.2	1 760.0	2 030.4	329.1	15.4
Dem. Rep. of the Congo	149.8	220.5	256.0	15.6	22.9	21.5	960.3	962.9	1 190.7	0.3	23.7
Ethiopia	88.0	89.0	88.0	9.2	9.3	8.2	956.5	957.0	1 073.2	0.0	12.1
Gambia	15.5	10.1	11.0	11.4	7.2	7.6	136.0	140.3	144.7	3.2	3.2
Ghana	163.5	103.6	111.6	5.6	3.3	3.4	2 919.6	3 139.4	3 282.4	7.5	4.6
Guinea	89.2	78.9	68.5	10.4	8.6	7.1	857.7	917.4	964.8	7.0	5.2
Guinea-Bissau	5.1	5.6	3.6	7.7	7.7	4.4	66.2	72.7	81.8	9.8	12.5
Guyana	46.5	37.9	36.2	6.8	5.4	5.2	683.8	701.9	696.2	2.6	-0.8
Honduras	234.4	197.6	197.9	9.7	8.3	8.0	2 416.5	2 380.7	2 473.8	-1.5	3.9
Madagascar	53.6	72.5	72.7	5.2	6.4	5.9	1 030.8	1 132.8	1 232.2	9.9	8.8
Malawi	66.9	38.9	50.6	13.6	7.5	9.3	491.9	518.7	544.1	5.4	4.9
Mali	59.5	63.0	66.1	5.0	4.9	4.8	1 190.0	1 285.7	1 377.1	8.0	7.1
Mauritania	54.1	60.0	60.8	13.7	14.1	13.4	394.9	425.5	453.7	7.8	6.6
Mozambique	47.1	50.9	57.3	4.0	3.0	3.0	1 177.5	1 696.7	1 910.0	44.1	12.6
Nicaragua	118.1	95.3	105.1	11.7	8.4	8.5	1 009.4	1 134.5	1 236.5	12.4	9.0
Niger	26.0	28.8	29.0	7.3	7.9	7.6	356.2	364.6	381.6	2.4	4.7
Rwanda	13.0	15.5	14.7	9.1	10.0	8.8	142.9	155.0	167.0	8.5	7.8
Sao Tome and Principe	3.2	2.1	1.1	13.7	8.2	4.1	23.4	25.6	26.8	9.6	4.8
Senegal	146.4	141.4	138.7	8.8	7.9	7.3	1 663.6	1 789.9	1 900.0	7.6	6.2
Sierra Leone	16.4	28.9	23.9	10.4	14.6	9.9	157.7	197.9	241.4	25.5	22.0
Uganda	75.5	85.5	91.5	9.6	9.8	9.2	790.6	876.9	994.6	10.9	13.4
United Rep. of Tanzania	99.8	128.6	148.4	5.8	6.8	7.3	1 720.7	1 891.2	2 032.9	9.9	7.5
Zambia	187.2	222.5	210.4	14.3	15.5	12.7	1 309.1	1 435.5	1 656.7	9.7	15.4
Sum/weighted average	**2 423.2**	**2 467.6**	**2 566.7**	**9.2**	**8.4**	**8.1**	**26 232.6**	**29 428.7**	**31 728.9**	**12.2**	**7.8**

Source: Data for debt service and debt service-to-exports are based on IMF and World Bank (2003a); the erroneous data for Uganda have been corrected with data provided in the 2002 Uganda DSA Update.

(b) Currency-specific short-term discount rates

The discount rates used to calculate the net present value (NPV)[46] are the currency-specific commercial interest reference rates (CIRRs) provided by the Organization for Economic Co-operation and Development (OECD) for its member countries' currencies, based on commercial lending rates.[47] These are called "short-term" CIRRs, as they represent an average for the six-month period before the reference date of the DSA. Currency-specific short-term CIRRs and NPV calculations raise two main issues.[48] The CIRRs give rise to arbitrary results regarding assistance levels and costs of the HIPC Initiative, while the NPV calculations are very sensitive to differences in discount rates. For example, in the case of a $10 million loan repayable at an interest rate of 4 per cent over 40 years (including a 10-year grace period), using a discount rate of 6 per cent results in an NPV of $7.5 million, while using a discount rate of 2 per cent results in an NPV of $13.9 million (nearly twice as much). In other words, every percentage point difference in the discount rate implies a change in the NPV of about 16 per cent.

The HIPC framework's use of these CIRRs entails the following problems:

(i) Currency-specific short-term CIRRs imply unfair burden sharing;

(ii) Averaging CIRRs over six months gives rise to high volatility in estimations of assistance and costs;

(iii) Averaging CIRRs over six months implies unfair assistance levels; and

(iv) The lack of clear rules as to what CIRR to use for non-OECD currencies has led to arbitrary use of discount rates.

Currency-specific discount rates imply highly unfair burden sharing whereby booming creditor countries are rewarded and creditor countries facing or recovering from recession are punished. This is because booming economies generally have higher CIRRs than countries in, or recovering from, a major recession. For example, the CIRR for the US dollar before the recent recession averaged around 6 per cent, while the CIRR for the yen during the recession in Japan averaged slightly above 2 per cent.

As interest rates change over time, any change in the DSA reference date implies changes in the discount rates and thus means changes in the NPV of HIPCs' debt and therefore HIPC debt relief. As Uganda's reassessment under the enhanced HIPC Initiative showed, high discount rates combined with overly optimistic export projections can make a country's debt appear sustainable, even though it is not.[49] Together with volatile exports (and/or volatile government revenues), the use of CIRRs in DSA results in highly unpredictable data that influence the costs and assistance levels of the HIPC Initiative. Averaging CIRRs over six months implies unfair assistance levels, as HIPCs assessed during periods of relatively high world interest rates will *ceteris paribus* receive less HIPC assistance than countries assessed during periods of relatively low world Interest rates.

The lack of clear rules as to what CIRR to use for non-OECD currencies has led to arbitrary use of discount rates in a number of cases. For example, the preliminary HIPC document for Tanzania (prepared in October 1999) used the CIRR of the SDR[50] for all currencies without an established CIRR; however, the preliminary HIPC document for Guinea (prepared in December 1999) used US dollar's CIRR (6.23 per cent) for the Chinese yuan, the French franc's CIRR (5.35 per cent) for currencies pegged to the French franc (and now pegged to the euro), and the CIRR of the SDR (5.25 per cent) for other currencies without an established CIRR. The use of OECD discount rates for non-OECD currencies is even inconsistent with the attempt to use interest rate differentials to determine the long-term value of currencies.

2. Do HIPCs actually save on debt service?

The extent to which there are debt service savings due to the HIPC initiative has been challenged, as HIPCs are not in a position to fully service their debt. For example, Cohen (2003) suggests that although the HIPC initiative has brought the average level of the debt-to-export ratio down from 300 per cent to 150 per cent, it is probable that the reduction merely eliminates the non-payable portion of the debt. Birdsall and Williamson (2002, p. 8) report that the United States Government — which is congressionally mandated to estimate the present value of its loan portfolio — applies a 92 per cent discount to the debt of HIPCs.

Chart 4 shows the actual total debt service payments of all 42 HIPCs, as well as of the 22 HIPCs that had reached their enhanced decision point by the end of 2000 (for which comprehensive and consistent data were available up to

Chart 4

TOTAL DEBT SERVICE PAID, 1990–2001

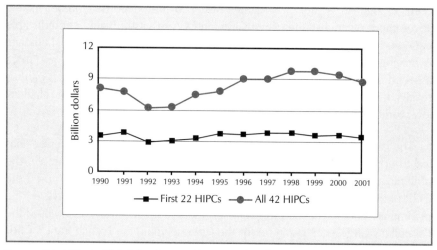

Source: World Bank, *Global Development Finance,* online data 2003.

2001). One key observation is that, compared to the early 1990s, the financial impact of the HIPC Initiative on actual total debt service payments is quite marginal. Indeed, actual debt service payments of the 22 HIPCs were slightly higher in 2001 than in 1992, 1993, and 1994. For a group of 27 HIPCs at the decision/completion point, debt service payments have been projected to increase steadily from about $2.4 billion to $2.6 billion between 2003 and 2005 (see tables 12a and 12b).

According to IMF and World Bank calculations, overall debt service of the above-mentioned 22 HIPCs has been cut by roughly one-third, compared with actual payments in the years immediately prior to the receipt of HIPC debt relief. However, these calculations neglect the fact that actual debt service payments in the years immediately prior to reaching decision points was higher than in earlier years, as HIPCs were not allowed to accrue arrears prior to reaching the decision point. For some HIPCs, such as Guinea-Bissau and Tanzania, donor countries provided grants to settle these arrears.

Considering that absolute numbers overstate the debt service burden, charts 5 and 6 show actual debt service payments as percentage ratios of exports and GDP respectively. It can be seen that there are some decreasing trends in the debt service burden relative to exports, though the source for this decreasing

Chart 5

TOTAL DEBT SERVICE PAID TO XGS, 1990–2001

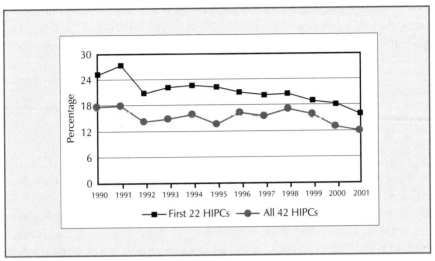

Source: Same as for chart 4.

Note: XGS - exports of goods and services.

Chart 6

TOTAL DEBT SERVICE PAID TO GDP, 1990–2001

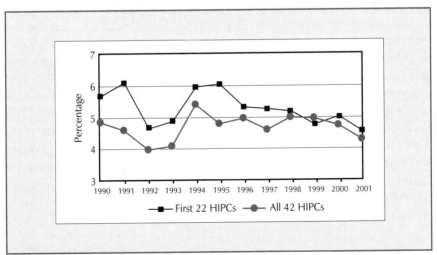

Source: Same as for chart 4.

debt service burden lies largely in increased exports.[51] While similar comprehensive data on government revenues are not available, there is some indication that government revenues grew much less than exports but slightly faster than GDP. Hence, the evolution of the debt service burden relative to government revenues is likely to be between the trends shown in charts 5 and 6.

(a) NPV debt reductions lead to continuously high debt service payments

The HIPC framework stipulates that each creditor is supposed to provide its share of HIPC debt relief, though it does not lay down how each creditor provides its debt relief, which is determined in terms of NPV debt reductions. Given that the key goal of the HIPC initiative is to provide a lasting solution to the problem of repeated debt rescheduling, its clear preference should have been to cancel either a part of the debt stock or at least a part of future debt service payments. However, due to political constraints of some creditors regarding these actions, it was agreed that creditors could provide their NPV debt relief through a rescheduling of debt service. Following previous Paris Club arrangements, this rescheduling applies also to repayments of ODA, which is rescheduled over 40 year (including a 16 year grace period) at original interest rates.

The main problem with such a rescheduling is that it actually increases the total debt service of a country in the long-term. Hence, though HIPC debt relief provided through rescheduling reduces debt service payments in the short term, it puts most debt service payments off to the future and will thus undermine long-term debt sustainability (especially if combined with overly optimistic growth rates, as is the case under the Initiative).[52] Unfortunately, this rescheduling problem is largely ignored or misinterpreted in the debt literature. A debt rescheduling may be appropriate for borrowers with temporary payment (i.e. liquidity) problems, but it is no solution for HIPCs' debt overhang, the causes of which are structural in almost all cases (i.e. insolvency). On the contrary, a debt rescheduling makes the situation worse for HIPCs, as it increases the cumulative amount of debt service payments.[53]

Chart 7 shows the projected annual debt service of the 27 decision-point HIPCs for 2003-2005.[54] Considering that nearly all of these 27 HIPCs are expected to have reached their completion point by the end of 2004, it is surprising to see that nominal debt service is projected to increase between 2003 and 2004. An examination of the weighted average debt service projections in terms of exports and government revenues (charts 8 and 9) reveals clearly declining trends, though at least part of these trends is due to overly optimistic growth rates for exports and government revenues. Furthermore, as table 13 shows, the picture looks far less promising for the remaining NPV debt levels of a number of individual HIPCs.

Chart 7

PROJECTED DEBT SERVICE ON PUBLIC EXTERNAL DEBT[a]

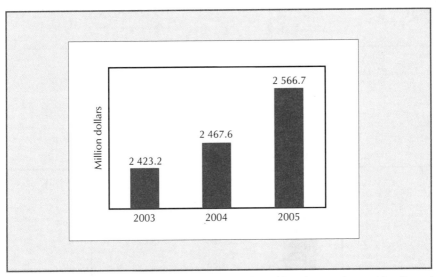

Source: Graphs created by UNCTAD based on IMF and World Bank (2003a); see tables 12a and 12b.

a 27 decision-point HIPCs, as of June 2003.

Chart 8

PROJECTED DEBT SERVICE ON PUBLIC EXTERNAL DEBT TO PROJECTED EXPORTS[a]

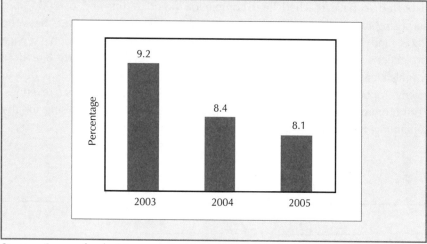

Source: Same as for chart 7.

   a   27 decision-point HIPCs, as of June 2003.

Chart 9

PROJECTED DEBT SERVICE ON PUBLIC EXTERNAL DEBT
TO PROJECTED GOVERNMENT REVENUES[a]

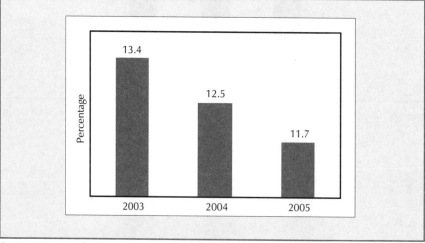

Source: Same as for chart 7.

   a   27 decision-point HIPCs, as of June 2003.

3. Is HIPC debt relief additional to traditional aid?

The official breakdown of the costs and benefits of the HIPC Initiative may be highly misleading, as it does not take into account the "true" allocation of costs and benefits. For example, if all creditors deducted the costs of HIPC debt relief from their traditional aid budgets for HIPCs, this would imply that the HIPCs were paying for the debt relief in terms of reduced traditional aid. The final costs to creditors would be zero, as would be the net benefits to HIPCs. Hence, in determining the true costs and benefits of the HIPC Initiative, it is necessary to make some decisions on how to allocate the costs of bilateral and especially of multilateral creditors to individual countries. This raises two important issues. First, is HIPC debt relief additional? And, second, will creditors make reallocations in their traditional aid budgets among the recipients of traditional aid due to the provision of HIPC debt relief?

Comparing data for the three years before the adoption of the HIPC Initiative (1994–1996) with data for the three years after the adoption of the HIPC Initiative (1997–1999), Gunter (2001) showed that there has been close to zero additionality, even for HIPCs that had reached their completion point. The World Bank's OED Review (Gautam, 2003) concluded that, even though there has been close to zero overall additionality, the most recent trends in aid flows indicate some aid reallocations towards eligible HIPCs.[55] As argued earlier, however, the World Bank concludes that: "All in all, the available data indicate a modest rise in total aid resources to HIPCs during the period of the Initiative." (World Bank, 2003, Box 6.2, p. 135). Considering that the HIPCs that have proceeded furthest with the Initiative have also advanced most with the implementation of their poverty reduction strategies, it could be argued that these "most successful" HIPCs received a higher share of aid than they had received in the past.

On the second question, it should be noted that most donor countries now provide the bulk of their foreign assistance in the form of grants. Thus, their ability to fund future aid programmes is not directly limited by the amount they receive back in repayments from prior loans. In the United States, for example, repayments for old foreign aid loans are treated as a miscellaneous receipt of the Treasury; and new appropriations would be needed to turn them into new loans. Debt forgiveness is funded by new appropriations. It should be noted that, until recently (2002), ODA levels were generally falling in parallel with new bilateral debt forgiveness.

In the case of the most relevant multilateral creditor, namely IDA, reflows account for about 40 per cent of current loanable resources. It is projected that they will increase to about 70 per cent in three decades due to previous agreements among IDA donors not to fully replenish IDA in real terms (for more details, see Sanford, 2004a; and GAO Report, 2004). Furthermore, given that IDA books the actual loss in HIPC loan repayments at the time in the future when the loan payment would have been received, it is pushing these costs to the future, with the hope that it will be reimbursed by donors at the time the losses in repayment are realized. As of June 2003, IDA already had an unfunded liability of $8.6 billion. Thus, unless it receives new funding commitments from donor countries, it would have to shrink its programme by that amount in future years. While IDA donors are currently discussing the question of how they will pay the costs of the existing HIPC programme, for example by making a major contribution now to endow a fund that would cover the lost reflows as they are realized, an immediate outlay of $6.9 billion is required. This, however, is unlikely to be forthcoming. The African Development Bank has a financing gap of at least $1 billion, while the Inter-American Development Bank is expected to finance its HIPC commitments at the expense of future lending. In conclusion, without new contributions from donor countries, it is likely that MFIs' concessional aid programmes will shrink in the future and most multilateral debt relief will not be additional.

Given that additionality for each eligible HIPC must be accurately accessed in order to estimate correctly the costs of the HIPC Initiative (which is impossible to determine, as it involves future decisions of creditors), Gunter and Wodon analysed two extreme cases: zero and full additionality. They allocated the full costs of bilateral debt relief to each bilateral creditor, but allocated the costs of multilateral debt relief on the basis of each country's share in world GDP. They concluded that, while most bilateral debt relief may be additional, the severe financing constraints of multilateral creditors are likely to force them to finance their costs through reductions in future multilateral aid, and the non-HIPC-eligible IDA countries would be likely to suffer reductions in aid (Gunter and Wodon, forthcoming).

Without doubt, in the absence of a counterfactual scenario, it is difficult to determine to what extent HIPC debt relief has been additional. What is clear from the analysis above, however, is that new mechanisms or initiatives are needed to attain a clear and significant level of additionality and to prevent an unfair reallocation of aid, particularly in the future, due to HIPC debt relief. As a recent 2003 HIPC Progress Report states:

> "There is also recognition by the international community that debt relief provided by the HIPC Initiative can reduce the debt burden significantly but not guarantee debt sustainability. For debt to remain at sustainable levels requires continued efforts by creditors, and debtors to ensure an appropriate level of concessionality of new resource flows, including through strengthening HIPC debt management capacity." (IMF and World Bank, 2003a, p. 29)

Unsustainable debt is generally associated with continuously increasing debt ratios over time. The analysis in this chapter suggests that even the claim that the HIPC Initiative is to "reduce the debt burden [of HIPCs] significantly" may have to be moderated in the light of projections of increasing debt service obligations (under highly optimistic growth and revenue projections) for the 27 HIPCs between 2003 and 2005. And while HIPCs could benefit from strengthening their debt management capacity, for example through programmes like the Debt Management and Financial Analysis System (DMFAS) of UNCTAD, they can do precious little to control exogenous shocks, which are critical in determining not only how much debt they contract in the first place, but also their debt servicing capacities. Sustainability of debt cannot be assessed in isolation, but must be seen within a holistic context of country-specific circumstances relating to the international trade and financial system and domestic development objectives. In Africa, the latter would include the attainment of the MDGs, in particular halving poverty by 2015. This underscores the need for creditors and donors to guarantee new resource flows in grant form at levels sufficient to meet the financing gaps (in terms of meeting the MDGs) not only of African HIPCs, but also of other equally poor and debt-distressed African countries.

Chapter IV

New approaches to attaining sustainable debt levels

"...And on current progress, we will fail to meet each Millennium Development Goal in Africa not just for 10 years but for 100 years. Far from achieving primary school education for all, 120 million children will still have no schools to go to, and the target will not be met in sub-Saharan Africa until 2150. Our targets to cut infant mortality by two thirds and halve poverty by 2015 will also go unmet in sub-Saharan Africa until 2150."

Gordon Brown, Chancellor of the Exchequer, United Kingdom, in <u>The Independent</u>, 1 June 2004, p. 29.

1. Introduction

Many suggestions have been made with a view to improving the HPIC Initiative as regards both sustainability and eligibility criteria. Yet some analysts have gone one step further to propose alternative debt relief modalities, such as payment caps on debt service or the human development approach centred on the level of financial resources that would enable HIPCs and other poor low-income developing countries to meet the MDGs.

2. Alternative modalities for delivering sustainable debt

(a) Payment caps on HIPC debt service

Limiting the debt service payments of HIPCs to 10 per cent (or 5 per cent for countries experiencing major public health emergencies) of internal revenues of

Governments is a prominent reform proposal, especially in the United States. In May 2003, the United States Congress passed a bill[56] requiring the Administration to seek agreement with other countries to put these limits on HIPC debt payments into effect.

The proponents of payment caps argue that the remaining high debt burden of HIPCs constitutes a challenge to the central objective of the HIPC Initiative "to provide a greater focus on poverty reduction by releasing resources for investment in health, education, and social needs."[57] Furthermore, it is contended that a cap on debt service payments would protect HIPCs against deteriorations in the world economy, as their debt payment obligations would be adjusted to the lower levels of government revenues. Without payment caps, HIPCs are likely to remain highly vulnerable to currency depreciations, as they would need to spend more of their revenues to purchase the foreign exchange necessary to service external debt. Thus, without a mechanism to automatically reduce countries' debt servicing obligations, HIPCs could find themselves in a situation where their debt burdens are once again unsustainable, even after full debt relief from the enhanced HIPC Initiative (see, especially, Kane, 2003).

Critiques of payment caps maintain, however, that the differences between the outcomes for HIPCs can be attributed as much to differences in the level of government revenues as to any variation in their treatment by the HIPC framework. Thus, a cap on debt service based on government revenue will benefit most those HIPCs whose Governments have the smallest share of revenues (relative to GDP) from domestic sources.[58] Such caps could, however, be defined with reference to historical values of government revenues, or in terms of GDP. While Birdsall and Williamson (2002) are not in favour of revenue-based payment caps, they suggest a maximum debt service-to-GDP ratio of 2 per cent in order to avoid rewarding low-revenue HIPCs.[59]

(b) The human development approach to debt sustainability

This approach was originally suggested by Northover, Joyner and Woodward at the Catholic Agency for Overseas Development (CAFOD) in 1998.[60] It argues that most of the world's poorest countries have unsustainable debt and that countries with a large proportion of their population living in absolute poverty have a more urgent need to spend their resources on poverty reduction than on debt service. It is for the same reason that other NGOs, such as OXFAM, Jubilee Research (formerly Jubilee 2000) and Debt Relief International, among others, have campaigned for a complete write-off of the debt of very poor low-income developing countries. Over the years, this campaign has won popular support in many developed countries.

The latest detailed proposal on the human development approach to debt relief is made by Berlage, Cassimon, Dreze, and Reding (2003). Recognizing that primary needs of human development are not met in many poor developing countries, and that the HIPC Initiative is not sufficient to resolve the debt overhang of these countries, they suggest a 15-year programme targeted at implementing the MDGs while eliminating all of the outstanding debt for a set of 49 poor countries. They argue that seven non-HIPCs with a 1997 Human Development Index below 0.5 (Bangladesh, Bhutan, Djibouti, Eritrea, Haiti, Nepal and Nigeria) should be added to the list of HIPCs in view of the fact that the concern for human development applies to all poor countries, heavily indebted or not.

(c) MDG-based approach to debt relief

There is increasing recognition that a full debt write-off will make an important contribution to reaching the MDGs in the current group of HIPCs and other poor debt-distressed African countries. However, as has been argued in previous UNCTAD reports (for example, UNCTAD, 2001, p. 26), even if all SSA's debt is written off, this would represent only half of the resource requirements for Africa's development in the next decade. Thus, a debt relief initiative that is premised on achieving the MDGs in all African HIPCs and other debt-distressed African countries, within the context of overall ODA flows to these countries, should be considered. The important benchmark for calculating the appropriate size of debt relief to be offered to this group of countries should be the level of resources that these countries need, taking into account the level of ODA flows, to attain the MDGs, without compromising growth.

High poverty and adverse social conditions have been identified as constraints on growth in all 11 African HIPCs[61] in the World Bank's OED Review (Gautam, 2003, annex I, pp. 87–88). As demonstrated in chapter I, continuing debt servicing by African countries would nominally constitute a reverse transfer of resources to creditors by a group of countries that by all indications could least afford this. Finally, Africa is the continent on which the MFIs, in particular the Bretton Woods institutions, have had the greatest influence in terms of policy-based lending replete with conditionalities. This is evidenced not only by the structural adjustment lending which increased manifold during the 1980s and 1990s, but also by the share of official bilateral debt (which was also predicated on such programmes) in total long-term outstanding debt (four-fifths during the period 2000–2002). Against this background, there should be a shared responsibility for Africa's debt overhang that would militate in favour of a write off.

3. Resource requirements

(a) Requirements for attaining MDGs

The difficult task of estimating the costs of meeting the MDGs (see box 1.2, World Bank, 2004, pp. 30–31) has been undertaken on the basis of two broad methodologies. One is based on global costing exercises with global elasticities and average cost guides, and the other is based on country-level estimates, with country-level information scaled up to the global level. Neither type of methodology, however, effectively incorporates the multisectoral dimension, which is addressed by two well-known studies: the Report prepared for the United Nations by the High-Level Panel on Financing for Development (known as the Zedillo Report (UN, 2001)) and a study at the World Bank by Devarajan et al. (2002).

In 2000, UNCTAD proposed doubling ODA for SSA and maintaining it at that level for at least a decade in order to create a virtual circle of growth and poverty reduction. The Zedillo report (UN, 2001), while finding UNCTAD's proposal for a doubling of ODA to SSA reasonable, estimates that roughly $50 billion a year in additional ODA will be required to achieve the MDGs in all developing countries, though it reiterates the difficulties of arriving at accurate estimates and notes that a more accurate and comprehensive estimate would need to be based on individual country estimates. Devarajan et al. (2002) use two different approaches. One approach estimates the MDG resource needs by calculating the economic growth rate of countries and the investment required to achieve the goals, while the second approach separately estimates the costs of achieving the individual goals. Both approaches yield comparable estimates of $40 to $60 billion per year in additional aid required to achieve the MDGs, although these estimates do not include certain costs, notably that of complementary infrastructure needed to attain such growth and investment rates.

(b) Meeting the costs of a debt write-off

Considering the annual cost of about $40–60 billion required to reach the MDGs in all developing countries, the cost of 100 per cent debt relief for all African HIPCs appears to be marginal. As shown in table 13, the total cost of forgiving all remaining debt of the 27 HIPCs that reached the decision/completion point by the end of 2003 amounts to about $29 billion in NPV terms (approximately $55 billion in nominal terms). Thus, with sufficient political will to back up total debt write-off, it should not be exceedingly difficult to fund the additional resources involved, including for non-HIPC but debt-distressed Africa countries. As argued by Susan George, for the debt crisis to vanish from the international scene, "it must be understood as a political rather than a financial phenomenon" (George, 1995). It is logical, therefore, to expect that the crisis will be more amenable to a "political solution" than to a financial one, as is the present case within the framework of the HIPC Initiative.

While some major donors have started to provide 100 per cent debt relief,[62] there remains a considerable amount of bilateral debt that HIPCs and other equally poor and debt-distressed African countries will find difficult to service. This situation is underscored by the persistence of critical developmental problems in these countries that discourage higher domestic and foreign investment. However, the current constraints in financing the MDG-based approach are enormous and might require a more constructive discussion that looks into new global financing instruments.

Resources for funding a complete write-off of Africa's multilateral debt could be raised through three possible channels: loan loss provisions, mobilization of donor resources for IFIs, or increased ODA flows.

Theoretically it is possible for the Bretton Woods institutions and other multilateral development banks to write off bad debts as their counterparts in

Table 13

REMAINING DEBT OF 27 HIPCS THAT REACHED THE ENHANCED DECISION POINT
BY END-2003

(Million dollars, NPV terms)

	Enhanced assistance in NPV terms	Percentage reduction in NPV terms	Remaining NPV debt
Benin	265	31	590
Bolivia	854	30	1 993
Burkina Faso*	324	49	334
Cameroon	1 260	27	3 407
Chad	170	30	397
Dem. Rep. of the Congo	6 311	80	1 578
Ethiopia	1 275	47	1 438
Gambia	67	27	181
Ghana	2 186	56	1 718
Guinea	545	32	1 158
Guinea-Bissau	416	85	73
Guyana	329	40	494
Honduras	556	18	2 533
Madagascar	814	40	1 221
Malawi	643	44	818
Mali	417	29	1 021
Mauritania	622	50	622
Mozambique	306	27	827
Nicaragua	3 267	72	1 271
Niger	521	54	444
Rwanda	452	71	185
Sao Tome and Principe	97	83	20
Senegal	488	19	2 080
Sierra Leone	600	80	150
Uganda	656	37	1 117
United Rep. of Tanzania	2 026	54	1 726
Zambia	2 499	63	1 468
Total	**27 966**	-	**28 861**

Source: HIPC Status Table (available on the HIPC website).

* The 129 million dollars Burkina Faso received as topping-up at the completion point have been added to the 195 million dollars of debt relief envisaged at the enhanced decision point.

the commercial banking sector do against loan loss provisions, but they have insisted that a complete debt write-off would negatively impact on their preferred creditor status and increase the cost of their own borrowing on capital markets. This has drawn some scepticism from certain observers. It is contended that their "preferred creditor status" does not appear to be based on any legal codes, but solely on the premise that in the event of default or external debt servicing problems, sovereign borrowers make preferential allocation of foreign exchange to service the debts owed to these institutions without triggering remedial action on the part of the other creditors. According to Adam Lerrick (of the Carnegie Melon University), total debt owed by the existing HIPCs amounts to only 5 per cent of IFIs' capital and 54 per cent of their provisions and reserves, and none of these institutions would find themselves in distress because of a 10 per cent fall in their equity capital. A total debt write-off for these countries will not, therefore, impair their ability to play an important role in the world economy (see Vasquez, 2001, pp. 24–49).

It is important to recall, however, that the earlier discussions on disaggregating the additional total costs of the Initiative to various creditors suggest that creditors, in particular some multilateral ones, are unlikely to provide further debt relief unless they receive assistance from donor countries. Thus, a complete write-off would only be possible if the main shareholders of the Bretton Woods institutions provide the additional funding to cover the share of these institutions (about 30 per cent of total debt stocks) in total debt relief for African HIPCs.

Indeed, the possibility of funding a complete debt write-off via aid resources should be explored, since aid levels are actually increasing, although slowly. After falling substantially in the second half of the 1990s, aid volumes rose in 2002. Net ODA flows, as estimated by the Development Assistance Committee (DAC) of the OECD, rose from $52.3 billion in 2001 to $58.3 billion in 2002. The ratio of ODA to donors' GNP, which fell from 0.34 per cent in the early 1990s to 0.22 per cent in 2001, rose to 0.23 per cent in 2002. Although the aid effort and new commitments vary widely across donors, aid volumes as a whole are set to rise further when DAC members begin to deliver on their Monterrey commitments. If these commitments are realized, total ODA would increase by about $18.5 billion over the 2002 level, from $58 billion to $77 billion, that is a 32 per cent rise in real terms, reaching 0.29 per cent of GNP in 2006.

While the increase in development assistance is encouraging, there are concerns that a large part of this increase may not finance the costs of meeting the MDGs. Of the roughly $6 billion nominal increase in ODA by DAC donors in 2002 (an approximately $4 billion increase in real terms), debt relief accounted for $2.9 billion, technical cooperation for $1.9 billion, and emergency and disaster relief and food aid for $0.7 billion. In terms of recipient country distribution, the increase in bilateral ODA was concentrated in a small number of countries. Indeed, there is some concern that additional aid flows, as well as their distribution, could be significantly influenced by donors' strategic agendas. It is important, therefore, to ensure that such strategic concerns, irrespective of their immediate importance to donors, should not crowd out development aid to the poorest low-income countries.

In any case, given that the real costs of debt relief can be spread over the lifetime of the remaining loans, which for multilateral loans is around 30 to 40 years, the annual cost of 100 per cent debt relief, at least for those HIPCs at the decision/completion point as at September 2003, remains relatively small in comparison to the resource requirements for meeting the MDGs.

It has often been argued that a 100 per cent debt write-off will send the wrong signals to debtor countries and others, set a bad precedent and thereby create a moral hazard for the IFIs. However, there is no greater moral hazard than the one entailed in constant restructuring and partial debt forgiveness based on creditors' perspectives and interests, as is the case under terms agreed with the Paris Club. On the contrary, moral hazard will be limited by dealing decisively with the recurring debt crisis of poor African countries through a truly permanent exit from constant rescheduling that establishes a basis for long-term debt sustainability for debtors within an appropriate framework of national and international policy measures. A complete debt write-off, therefore, becomes a "moral imperative", as it will guarantee resources to help meet the MDGs in Africa and assure an exit from the debt crisis for the continent. UNCTAD has suggested that the international community consider applying key insolvency principles to international debt work-outs and writing off all unpayable debt in SSA determined on the basis of an independent assessment of debt sustainability (see UNCTAD, 1998, p. xii).

4. Addressing specific design problems in the HIPC Initiative

In the absence of political will for a debt write-off, the HIPC Initiative should be improved in the light of its implementation and design problems discussed earlier, if it is to be credible. This section examines some of the issues that might have to be addressed to improve the Initiative, namely: (i) inappropriate eligibility and debt sustainability indicators, which, for example, exclude domestic debt; (ii) the use of overly optimistic growth projections; (iii) insufficient interim debt relief; (iv) problems in the delivery of HIPC debt relief, (v) the limitations of the burden-sharing concept; and (vi) inappropriate use of discount rates for the calculation of NPV.

(a) Revisions to HIPC eligibility and debt sustainability indicators

The narrow IDA/PGRF-only criterion could be replaced with UNDP's Human Poverty Index for developing countries (HPI-1). A practical complement to this would be some fiscal sustainability criterion, which would necessitate taking account of vulnerability factors, such as export concentration and export price volatility, as these have considerable fiscal implications for most HIPCs and other very poor low-income developing countries.[63]

Specifically, improving the fiscal sustainability criteria might involve eliminating the two threshold ratios for the applicability of the fiscal window (i.e. the minimum requirements of having an export-to-GDP ratio of 30 per cent and a government revenue-to-GDP ratio of 15 per cent).[64] Also, more emphasis could be given to fiscal debt sustainability criteria,[65] while the emphasis on the inappropriate NPV debt-to-export criterion could be reduced. A combination of an NPV debt-to-GDP indicator[66] and an NPV debt-to-government revenue indicator could be used, together with poverty levels and vulnerability factors to assess a HIPC's long-term debt sustainability, which could then form the basis for determining the cumulative amount of debt relief due to each HIPC. An appropriately defined debt service-to-government revenue indicator (together with a set of criteria for necessary investments in anti-poverty programmes) could be used to determine the maximum annual debt service payments that each HIPC can bear.[67] Debt sustainability analysis would have to take account of domestic debt in view of its broader macroeconomic but in particular fiscal impact on the poorest countries.

Some improvement in the fiscal sustainability criteria could also be attained by using a much longer backward-looking average, ending with the year before the initiative was adopted (1995), to calculate government revenues, instead of the current practice of using a three-year backward-looking average ending with the year previous to the decision/completion point. Finally, considering the necessity of deepening debt relief for the poorest countries, the NPV debt-to-revenue ratio should be reduced.[68]

(b) Overly optimistic growth projections

In the case of growth rates of exports, projections would be more realistic if the impact of export price volatility, the extent of diversification of exports, and a variety of other structural factors were taken into account. Projections of future economic growth rates should rely more on historical growth rates for each country. Furthermore, considering that the amount of debt relief provided would need to be sufficient to convince private investors that a country is likely to remain debt-sustainable in the foreseeable future, the lower bounds of realistic growth projections should be used in calculating sustainable debt levels.

(c) Insufficient interim debt relief

Considering that most creditors have failed to provide levels of interim debt relief that could make a significant difference to poverty reduction programmes in countries at the decision point, such relief would need to be scaled up considerably. A common misunderstanding is that higher interim debt relief would increase the costs of the HIPC Initiative, but this is not correct, as the total amount of HIPC debt relief is fixed in NPV terms.[69] The amount of interim debt relief provided should also take into consideration the costs of servicing HIPCs' domestic debt, most of which is short-term and thus implies a high fiscal burden, especially during the interim period. Indeed, in the interim period HIPCs could be encouraged to use a proportion of debt relief resources to retire domestic debt as a means of easing the fiscal burden.

(d) Adjustments in the burden-sharing concept

Most multilateral debt relief (excluding that of the IMF) is financed by bilateral donors, partly through contributions to the HIPC Trust Fund and partly through direct contributions to multilateral development banks (MDBs) in the form of replenishments (like IDA replenishments).[70] An immediate release of the HIPC Trust Fund resources would be likely to allow the full participation of the currently non-participating MDBs. According to the 2003 HIPC Status Report, the total cost to all non-participating MDBs together would amount to $72 million in 2002 NPV terms (IMF and World Bank, 2003a, table 8, p. 86), which is a marginal amount compared to the $1.7 billion that bilateral donors have thus far paid into (or pledged to) the Trust Fund.

The issue of HIPC creditors could be addressed in the following manner: payment into a Trust Fund of the amount of debt relief that a HIPC creditor is supposed to provide, financed from the amount of debt relief that the HIPC creditor is to receive from its creditors. This option has two major advantages over other options: first the financial impact will be exactly the same for all creditors and debtors as that of the current burden-sharing concept; and second, the costly negotiations and litigations of HIPCs against HIPCs would be avoided. A second option is the incorporation of a "de minimis" clause into the HIPC Initiative, which would be consistent with existing Paris Club regulations, exempting minor creditors from the provision of HIPC debt relief. As with the first option, however, HIPC debtors would be penalized with a reduction in total debt relief, which could probably be financed from Trust Fund resources as suggested in option two.

Finally, it is worth considering the introduction of a centralized consultation mechanism, possibly through the United Nations, in order to bring all creditors on board. These consultations could be with: (i) bilateral creditors that are not members of the IMF and the World Bank; (ii) bilateral creditors that have a history of not participating in traditional debt relief; and (iii) all commercial creditors. While such negotiations might not necessarily lead to the provision of full HIPC debt relief, some creditors would almost certainly provide more debt relief than under the current practice based more or less on moral suasion.

(e) Using a single fixed low discount rate
for the NPV calculation

There is no way to predict accurately the long-term values of currencies, and it would therefore be more pragmatic to use one fixed discount rate for the NPV calculation of all debt, irrespective of the currency in which a particular debt is denominated. A major advantage of this is the elimination of the problems associated with the current methodology of currency-specific short-term discount rates discussed in chapters II and III. It might also be possible to discard the concept of NPV of debt, as there are some indications that several investors are not as concerned about the NPV of a country's debt as they are about its nominal value. However, as this might entail some injustice in the provision of debt relief to countries with sharply diverging maturity structures, as well as some unfairness for creditors providing debt relief on debts with different levels of concessionality, some reasonable level of discounting might seem appropriate. For example, one relatively low level discount rate, such as 3 per cent, could be used for all currencies.

Conclusions

The analysis illustrates the weaknesses of the HIPC approach with respect to finding a permanent exit solution to the debt crisis of African HIPCs, and highlights the fact that several other equally poor African countries have been left out of the process. On the question of the level of debt deemed to be sustainable for countries the majority of whose population lives on less than one or two dollars a day per person, the answer is self-evident: considering the seriousness with which the international community is addressing the attainment of the MDGs, these targets should be used as a major benchmark for debt sustainability. This in turn implies that virtually all of the outstanding debt would need to be written off, as the resources needed to attain these goals are substantial.

It is contended that a write-off of the debt of the poorest countries may represent a "moral hazard" and discourage economic reforms by debtors, and that it may affect the status that the international financial institutions enjoy as "preferred creditors". These are legitimate questions and must be taken into consideration. At the same time, however, it could be counter-argued that since the poor countries, particularly in Africa, would have to continue to rely on greatly increased levels of ODA to reduce poverty and attain the MDGs, there is little likelihood of their abandoning economic reform. Furthermore, as shown earlier, a write-off of the debt of poor African countries is unlikely to cause financial distress to the IFIs, as the amount involved is relatively small compared with their capital and could thus be absorbed through loan loss provisions, as is the practice in the commercial banking sector.

In the absence of the political will for debt cancellation, the international community could consider applying the principles of bankruptcy codes to international debt work-outs corresponding to the notion of insolvency under such codes. For this process not to be unduly influenced by the interests of creditors, it could be undertaken by an independent expert body that would adjudicate on the basis of a more comprehensive set of criteria for debt sustainability, including that of meeting the MDGs.

Finally, at issue is whether providing a permanent exit solution to the debt overhang of these poor countries is a moral imperative. Much of the debt, particularly of countries that were of geopolitical strategic interest, is considered "odious" by many observers. Moreover, the huge increase in multilateral lending has been in the context of structural adjustment policies applied in the past 20 years, which have failed to engender the expected sustainable growth in Africa. Hence, there would appear to be some need for shared responsibility in terms of resolving Africa's debt crisis.

That Africa's debt burden has been a major obstacle to the region's prospects for economic growth and investment and poverty reduction is not in doubt. The continent's debt overhang has frustrated public investment in physical and social infrastructure, and therefore deterred private investment. And by undermining critical investments in health and human resource development, the debt overhang has compromised some of the essential conditions for sustainable economic growth and development and poverty reduction. There is now a consensus that, for a permanent solution to the external debt crisis, African countries would need to pursue policies of prudent debt management, economic diversification and sustained economic growth, which would require greater policy space. Equally, there is a consensus that the international community has to support these national policies with concerted and coherent actions in the areas of trade and finance through increased market access and major reductions, and eventually elimination, of agricultural subsidies, combined with international action on commodities, and increased ODA. It is only through this partnership that African countries would be able to achieve sustained high growth rates and development, implement the poverty reduction strategies necessary to meet the development challenges facing the continent, and attain the MDGs, in particular that of halving poverty by 2015.

Notes

1   Gordon Brown and Jim Wolfensohn, "A new deal for the world's poor", *The Guardian* (2004).

2   Of the 50 African countries for which there are data over the period 2000–2002, private non-publicly guaranteed debt as a percentage of total debt was significant for only two countries, at about 30 per cent (Mozambique and South Africa); for three other countries, Morocco, Tunisia, and Côte d'Ivoire, the proportion was 9, 10, and 12 per cent, respectively. Over the same period, private debt was below 5 per cent of total debt stock for 11 countries, and the rest of the countries had no private debt at all.

3   For instance, Nigeria is a heavily indebted country with an NPV debt-to-export ratio of 188 per cent (above the 150 per cent threshold) and a per capita income of about $300, which is less than half the limit of $875 for eligible countries. However, Nigeria is not eligible for HIPC assistance because, as a 'blend country', it cannot access International Development Association (IDA) assistance for poverty reduction purposes.

4   For a detailed discussion of the genesis of the debt crisis in developing countries as whole, see UNCTAD, 1988, chapter IV, pp. 91–131.

5   In circumstances where the private sector was unwilling to accept (political) risks, the motivation for commercial lending or guaranteeing of such loans to these countries by industrial country Governments was to stimulate their own exports in order to achieve economic benefits in terms of protecting or creating domestic employment and benefits of consolidating diplomatic relations ("national interest"). Many official creditor Governments also saw the provision of commercially priced export credit guarantees as a complement to direct grants and concessional ODA in their overall development cooperation policy, as most low-income developing countries were aid recipients (Daseking and Powell, 1999, p. 4).

6   Arrears owed by North African countries amounted to just $288 million in 1995.

7   The notion of "odious debt" (i.e. debts that were contracted by illegitimate Governments and should arguably be forgiven) dates back to the Spanish-American War, where the United States argued that Cuba's debt was odious as it was incurred without the consent of the people and did not benefit the people (see IMF 2003, p. 16). In the case of Africa, it has been argued that debts contracted by former dictators, in particular during the Cold War rivalries, should be regarded as "odious" and therefore written off.

8   The various terms agreed for debt relief (or rescheduling) are named after the major proponent of the terms (e.g. Nicholas F. Brady, the US Secretary of the Treasury in 1989) or after the city in which the meeting of the Group of Seven leading industrialized countries (G7)(now G8) held their annual meeting to approve of the terms and at which (or shortly after which) the Paris Club agreed to the new terms of debt relief. Under the Brady Plan, debtor countries with ongoing structural adjustment programmes with the IMF and the World Bank were eligible to participate in three broad instruments: debt buy-backs, exchange of old debts at a discount for new collateralized bonds; and exchange of old debt for new par value bonds, but at reduced interest rates. Commercial banks provided new money to finance these transactions, while creditor Governments gave relief through the Paris Club of official bilateral creditors.

9 Seehttp://www.clubdeparis.org/en/presentation/presentation.php?BATCH =B01WP04.

10 Since short-term debt is usually only reprofiled, it does not benefit from debt reduction.

11 Debt and development problems of developing countries, adopted by the Trade and Development Board at its ninth special session on 11 March 1978.

12 See the description of the HIPC Initiative on the HIPC website (http:// www.worldbank.org/hipc/).

13 The understanding was that the requirement for the six-year record of satisfactory performance would be implemented on a case-by-case basis, and countries could receive credit for the decision point stage for programmes already under way.

14 The NPV of debt is calculated using a discount rate, which in the case of the HIPC Initiative is picked from the OECD's six-month commercial interest reference rates (CIRRs). The CIRRs are commercial interest reference rates compiled and published by the OECD. They may be applied under the OECD arrangements on Guidelines for officially supported export credits, and are provided in the table on discount and exchange rates in all HIPC Decision Point documents. The rates used for HIPC debt are average CIRRs for the currencies concerned over the six-month period ending at the cut-off point for debt data (usually end-June or end-December). The CIRR of the Special Drawing Right (SDR) — calculated on the basis of its composite currencies' CIRRs — is used as a proxy for all currencies for which the CIRRs are not available.

15 See Perspectives on the Current Framework and Options for Change – Further Supplement on Costing (May 12, 1999), table 4; available on the HIPC website.

16 The poverty reduction strategy paper provides a more explicit link between debt relief and appropriate macroeconomic, structural and social policies. It is prepared by national authorities in close collaboration with the World Bank and IMF staff and is expected to enhance country ownership of HIPCs' economic adjustment and reform programmes in line with the objective of being "country-driven, and developed transparently with broad participation of elected institutions, stakeholders, including civil society, key donors, and regional banks; include monitorable outcome indicators; and have a clear link with the agreed Millennium Development Goals for 2015 (IMF Pamphlet Series – No.5: "*The Enhanced HIPC Initiative*", pp.33). See UNCTAD (2002a) for a critical review of PRSPs.

17 The problems associated with the implementation of macroeconomic policy reforms, and the design and implementation of PRSPs, which are conditions for reaching completion point, are the subject of a critical analysis in UNCTAD's *Report on Economic Development in Africa* (see UNCTAD, 2002a).

18 An interim PRSP (I-PRSP) could serve as a substitute for a blueprint to get to decision point pending the preparation of a full PRSP.

19 Available data for the IMF and the World Bank do not distinguish between interim relief and completion point relief. As at the end of May 2003, the World Bank had delivered 25 per cent or more of total committed debt service reduction in only two cases, but as at the end of July 2003, the IMF had disbursed 100 per cent of the debt relief committed in six completion point countries (Bolivia, Mali, Mauritania, Mozambique, Tanzania and Uganda) and more than 50 per cent in four additional cases (See IMF and World Bank HIPC country documents and World Bank Staff estimates, 2003, and IMF Finance Department (http://www.imf.org/external/fin.htm)).

20 This total cost excludes that of Liberia, Somalia, Sudan and Lao PDR due to data problems and in some cases protracted arrears.

21 A detailed discussion of these issues is provided by Cline, 1997.

22 The AfDB, for example, is the largest recipient of the Trust Fund's resources and is likely to continue to be, as donors are expected to finance about 90 per cent of the debt relief provided by it. (Of the total debt relief costs to the African Development Bank Group of $3.3 billion (2002 NPV), its own internal contribution towards this amounts to $370 million.) Indeed, it is explicitly stated in the debt relief agreements signed between the AfDB and HIPCs that the provision of debt relief is conditional on the availability of resources. This protects the financial integrity of the Bank Group while at the same time shifting the burden of financing debt relief to donors, who gave it political assurances at a donors' meeting held in Paris in June 2000 to fill any financing gap that the Bank Group might face in providing its share of debt relief.

23 Debt relief agreements between Malawi, Guinea and Zambia (decision point countries) and their non-Paris Club creditors (NPCs), for instance, have yet to be signed. Mauritania reached its completion point (June 2002) before the negotiation process to deliver debt service relief by its NPCs began; and as of September 2003, the country had yet to receive any debt service relief from these creditors.

24 The claims of creditor litigations are usually a multiple of the official HIPC costs, and the costs for HIPCs to engage or settle these litigations are high. While the IMF and World Bank have now pledged to help HIPCs with the litigations they face, not only does this help come a little bit late, it is still provided on a case-by-case basis (instead of through coordinated and concerted action).

25 While the membership of the IMF and IDA include some 180 countries, most of the developing countries' voting power is so marginal that they are de facto excluded from the decision making process. For recent reform proposals of the IMF voting power, see Buira (2002).

26 Debt buyback is the other approach employed by HIPCs in securing debt relief from Non-Paris Club members and other non-participating creditors.

27 The nine African countries are Burundi, Central African Republic, Comoros, Congo, Côte d'Ivoire, Liberia, Somalia, Sudan and Togo.

28 Indeed, considering the heavy cost of this arrangement to the African Development Bank in particular, it was agreed that this financing arrangement was exceptional and should not be seen as a precedent for other HIPCs with chronic arrears problems.

29 While the World Bank Operational Policies stipulate that countries are eligible for IDA on the basis of (a) relative poverty and (b) lack of creditworthiness, the operational cut-off for IDA eligibility for FY2004 is a 2002 per capita GNI of $865, using the World Bank Atlas methodology. In exceptional circumstances, IDA extends eligibility to countries such as small island economies that are above the operational cut-off.

30 The human poverty index for developing countries (HPI-1) is a composite index that measures deprivations in the three basic dimensions captured in the human development index: long and healthy life (probability at birth of not surviving to age 40); knowledge (adult literacy rate); and a decent standard of living (percentage of people without sustainable access to an improved water source and the percentage of children under age five underweight for their age). This gives a broader view of a country's level of development than income alone.

31 See, for example, footnote 1 of Claessens, Detragiache, Kanbur, and Wickham (1997) for the original list of HIPCs, which included Nigeria.

32 Formally, Bolivia acquired blend status, i.e. it is eligible for both IDA and IBRD resources, as of 1 July 2001 (see IDA, 2001, p. 7).

33 The level of government revenues for 2003 is calculated based on data for debt service and debt service-to-government revenues provided in table 3 of the 2003 HIPC Progress Report (IMF and World Bank, 2003a, pp. 79-81). Thereafter, the NPV debt-to-revenue ratios in 2003 (with and without HIPC debt relief) were calculated combining the data on projected government revenues with the NPV assistance levels and the percentage reductions in NPV debt.

34 The African countries in the survey were: Burundi, Uganda, Gambia, Ghana, Malawi, Sierra Leone, Lesotho, Nigeria, Cape Verde, Zambia, Rwanda, Kenya, Namibia, Swaziland and South Africa. Other countries in the survey consisted of Mexico, Brazil, Lithuania, Italy, India and New Zealand, were also included in the survey.

35 The NPV calculation sums up all future debt service obligations, with future debt service obligations being discounted depending on when the debt service is due.

36 For example, the European Union's Maastricht Treaty (signed in early 1992) limited the ratio of government debt to GDP to 60 per cent, though it was also agreed that higher ratios would be acceptable as long as the debt to GDP ratio was falling sufficiently over time. Indeed, most countries of the EU had a debt to GDP ratio above 60 per cent for most of the times during the 1990s, and at least three countries (Belgium, Greece, and Italy) had debt to GDP ratios of more than 100 per cent. However, it should be stressed that the Maastricht Treaty's debt to GDP ratio should not be interpreted as a debt sustainability indicator, but as a convergence criterion set by a group of European countries that intended to adopt a single currency by the end of 2001.

37 For example, the debt service-to-export ratio has recently been used as one of four indicators for the eighth Millennium Development Goal (MDG-8), whereby a target of 15 per cent is regarded as "Deal[ing] comprehensively with the debt problems of developing countries through national and international measures in order to make debt sustainable in the long term." The four indicators for this target are (a) the proportion of official bilateral HIPC debt cancelled, (b) debt service as a percentage of exports of goods and services, (c) the proportion of ODA provided as debt relief, and (d) the number of countries reaching HIPC decision and completion points.

38 The difference between GDP and GNP is due to net factor payments, which are defined as factor payments of foreigners active in the domestic economy minus factor payments to nationals active abroad. There also are small statistical discrepancies between GDP and GDI, as the statistical bases for the two measurements (on the product and income sides) are different from one another. The same applies for the statistical discrepancy between GNP and GNI.

39 Re-exports were usually included in the export figures, though they have more recently been excluded, especially in cases where re-exports were considered to be substantial.

40 See IMF, External Evaluation of the Enhanced Structural Adjustment Facility (ESAF), Report by a Group of Independent Experts, June 1998, pp. 39-40 (http://www.imf.org/external/pubs/ft/extev/index.htm).

41 Data related to Kenya's domestic public debt and most fiscal data have been taken from the external website of the Central Bank of Kenya (http://www.centralbank.go.ke)

42 Nigeria graduated from the IDA-only category in 1965.

43 As a World Bank (2000, p. 3) report pointed out, "Poverty, unemployment and low education feed into conflict and are a more important cause of it than ethnic diversity."

44 While the empirical debt overhang literature goes back to the early 1990s (see Gunter (2002) for a list of the main initial contributions), many of the latest empirical studies were presented at a UNU/WIDER conference on debt relief in September 2001; see especially Bigsten, Levin, and Persson (2001), Chowdhury (2001), Dijkstra and Hermes (2001), Hansen (2001), Pattillo, Poirson and Ricci (2002), Serieux and Samy (2001) and Were (2001).

45 For example, if the enhanced decision point is in December 2000, the DSA is likely to be based on relevant data as of December 1999 (if the country's fiscal year coincides with the calendar year) or June 2000 (if the country's fiscal year goes from July to June).

46 In order to understand the significance of this concept, consider the example of two country cases. Country A has nominal outstanding debt of $100 million, which is all due in the next year. Country B has nominal outstanding debt of $120 million, which is interest-free and due in 10 years. Which country would you prefer to be? While country A's nominal debt (100 million) is lower than country B's nominal debt (120 million), the fact that country B has no principal and no interest due for the next 10 years makes country B's debt far more attractive. Indeed, the NPV of country A's debt would be $100 million, while the NPV of country B's debt would be less than $70 million (using a discount rate of 6 per cent).

47 The CIRR of the Special Drawing Right (SDR) is calculated on the basis of its composite currencies' CIRRs.

48 The use of currency-specific discount rates suffers from two main weaknesses, which render them unsuitable for the calculation of NPV. First, the future interest rate differentials of currencies for the remaining repayment periods are unknown. Also, one cannot accurately forecast whether these future interest rate differentials would appropriately reflect differences in future currency values (as the theory of interest rate parity suggests). Linked to this is the deep-seated belief that currencies of developing countries are less stable than OECD currencies, although there is no objective way to quantify such differences. While historical trends of devaluations may give some indications, the past weaknesses of a currency do not necessarily imply future devaluations.

49 Uganda's original completion-point DSA showed that its NPV debt-to-export ratio at the end of June 1999 would be 207 per cent. On the other hand, Uganda's enhanced decision-point DSA showed that the actual NPV debt-to-export ratio was 240 per cent.

50 The Special Drawing Right (SDR) is the IMF's standard unit of account, introduced in 1969. IMF member countries may use SDRs to settle international trade balances and debts if the member country meets a variety of conditions. The SDR's value is currently based on a basket of the US Dollar, the Japanese yen, the British pound, and the euro.

51 The 42 HIPCs more than doubled the value of their exports from $35 billion in 1990 to over $73 billion in 2001. Although their share of world exports declined steadily

from 0.69 per cent (1990) to 0.55 per cent (1995), it has since then risen to 0.81 per cent in 2001 (Gunter, 2003, p. 28).

52 Another technical problem is that the rescheduling of ODA debt repayments does not usually provide much NPV debt reduction. In cases where the original interest rate on ODA is higher than the discount rate, the rescheduling of repayments of ODA debt actually increases the NPV. The burden to achieve the overall NPV debt reduction thus falls on non-ODA debt. In addition to the problem of a large portion of non-eligible debt, this has in some cases contributed to a result whereby a complete cancellation of all "eligible debt" has not been sufficient to reach the required NPV debt reduction.

53 Note that Easterly's (1999) characterization that substantial debt relief has been provided to HIPCs before the HIPC Initiative is misleading as: (a) a large part of traditional debt relief involved rescheduling (providing an NPV debt reduction but no debt relief on the total debt service); and, (b) traditional debt relief was only provided on eligible debt (pre-cut-off-date and non-ODA debt).

54 Comparing chart 7 data with chart 4 seems to indicate a considerable drop in debt service payments between 2001 and 2003; however, most of this drop is due to differences in data definitions. The Global Development Finance data shown in charts 4-6 refer to total external debt service, while debt service shown in charts 8-9 refers to debt service on external public and publicly guaranteed debt.

55 It could be argued that the analysis of the 2003 HIPC Progress Report, which examines gross and net flows of official external resources from 1997 to 2002, is not realistic as it includes countries like the Democratic Republic of Congo and Rwanda, which, due to civil conflicts, did not receive much aid in the late 1990s.

56 On 27 May, the President of the United States signed the bill HR. 1298, *the United States Leadership Against HIV/AIDS, Tuberculosis, and Malaria Act of 2003* (Public Law 108-25), after it had been passed by the House and Senate. It requires the Secretary of the Treasury to seek agreement with other major international financial institution members on changes in the HIPC initiative. Enough debt should be forgiven to reduce debt payments within three years to no more than 150 per cent of exports, and the annual payment due on public and publicly guaranteed debt should be no more than 10 per cent of a Government's annual revenue from internal sources (5 per cent for countries suffering a public health crisis). The Bill states that other benchmarks, such as a percentage of GNP, could be used if they yield substantially equivalent results (see Sanford and Gunter, 2004).

57 See the 1999 G-7 Communiqué, available on the HIPC website. Indeed, Loko, Mlachila, Nallari, and Kalonji (2003, p. 17) have concluded that: "External debt affects poverty not only through its negative impact on public investment and income growth but also through high debt service's crowding out of governments' social spending. High debt service directly reduces government budgetary allocations on health, education, social safety nets, and water and sanitation, in part because governments find it politically easier to cut back spending in such sectors because the poor are not usually organized to have a voice in such decisions." By contrast, others have argued that HIPC debt payments do not crowd out social programmes and that — even with 100 per cent forgiveness — the HIPCs could not increase their spending much faster (effectively and without waste).

58 For example, Birdsall and Williamson (2002, p. 86) ask: "Does one really want to reward countries for failing to get their citizens to pay a reasonable level of taxes?"

59 However, it should be pointed out that it is largely inaccurate to portray HIPCs with low government revenue-to-GDP ratios as inefficient, as low government revenues are most often due to structural and historical reasons.

60 See Northover (2001) and EURODAD (2002) for more details.

61 These are Burkina Faso, Cameroon, Côte d'Ivoire, Ethiopia, Ghana, Malawi, Mozambique, Tanzania, Togo, Uganda and Zambia.

62 For example, Switzerland provides all its aid to the least developed countries in the form of grants and cancelled any remaining bilateral debt many years ago. Some Paris Club creditors (Australia, Canada, Denmark, Italy, the United Kingdom and the United States) have indicated that they will provide 100 per cent debt relief to HIPCs after the enhanced completion point is reached. Austria, Belgium, France, Germany, Japan and the Netherlands have indicated that they will provide 100 per cent debt relief on all debts excluding post-cut-off-date non-ODA debt.

63 These vulnerability factors were deleted from the debt sustainability criteria of the enhanced HIPC framework for the sake of simplifying it.

64 While it is argued that the thresholds are justified to provide some incentives for countries to increase their exports-to-GDP and revenue-to-GDP ratios, as argued earlier (see chapters II and III), it needs to be borne in mind that ratios below the thresholds usually reflect structural problems, which are unlikely to be overcome in the short term. Furthermore, given that countries are required to have undergone at least three years of "successful" adjustment supported by the Bank and the Fund before reaching the HIPC decision point, it is difficult to argue (a) that further incentives are needed to determine HIPC eligibility and/or (b) that without these thresholds, the HIPC Initiative would reward inefficient countries.

65 The recommendation to focus more on government revenue-related indicators is not new. For example, nearly 15 years ago, Dittus (1989) analysed the budgetary dimension of the debt crisis in low-income sub-Saharan Africa and suggested that the debt service-to-revenue ratio be assigned a central role.

66 As Birdsall and Williamson (2002) pointed out, a debt criteria based on GDP would avoid rewarding countries for having failed to collect taxes. However, there is no need to make this the only criteria.

67 This builds on a recent suggestion made by EURODAD (2002) calling for a country-by-country analysis of how much debt each country can afford to carry without pre-empting resources available for spending on a basic level of social service delivery.

68 Some critiques have argued against deepening HIPC debt relief on the grounds that the majority of the world's poor people live in countries that are not eligible for HIPC debt relief. However, this simply reflects, or confirms, the inappropriateness of the HIPC eligibility criteria and should not constitute an argument against deeper debt relief.

69 Thus, the point of time at which HIPC debt relief is provided is not important for the creditor, except in those cases where HIPCs benefiting from interim relief fail to reach completion, the chances of which are low considering the HIPC policy conditionalities that must be implemented in the interim period and the promise of irrevocable debt relief at completion.

70 A thorough discussion of these issues is provided by Cline (1997).

References

AfDB (2000). *Annual Report 1999*, Report by the Boards of Directors of the African Development Bank and the African Development Fund covering the period 1 January to 31 December 1999.

AfDB (2002). *Annual Report 2001*, Report by the Boards of Directors of the African Development Bank and the African Development Fund covering the period 1 January to 31 December 2001.

Balassa B (1981). The Newly Industrializing Developing Countries after the Oil Crisis. *Weltwirtschaftliches*, Archiv, Band 117, Heft 1: 142–194.

Balassa B (1985). Exports, Policy Choices and Economic Growth in Developing Countries after the First Oil Shock. *Journal of Development Economics*, 18: 23–35.

Beaugrand P, Loko B and Mlachila M (2002). The Choice Between External and Domestic Debt in Financing Budget Deficits: The Case of Central and West African Countries. *IMF Working Paper* WP/02/79. Washington, DC.

Berlage L, Cassimon D, Dreze, J and Reding, P (2003). Prospective Aid and Indebtedness Relief, A Proposal. *World Development* 31 (10): 1635–54.

Bigsten A, Levin J, and Persson H (2001). Debt Relief and Growth, A Study of Zambia and Tanzania. United Nations University/World Institute for Development Economics Research (UNU/WIDER), Discussion Paper 2001/104 (www.wider.unu.edu/publications/dps/dp2001-104.pdf).

Bird G and Milne A (2003). Debt Relief for Low Income Countries, Is it Effective and Efficient? *The World Economy* 26 (1): 43–59.

Birdsall N, and Williamson J with Deese B (2002). Delivering on Debt Relief, From IMF Gold to a New Aid Architecture. Center for Global Development and Institute for International Economics, Washington, DC.

Brooks R, Cortes M, Fornasari F, Ketchekmen B, Metzgen, Y, (1998). External Debt Histories of Ten Low-income Developing Countries: Lessons from their Experience, IMF Working Paper 98/72, International Monetary Fund, Washington, DC.

Brown G and Wolfensohn J, (2004). "A new deal for the world's poor", *The Guardian*, 16 February.

Buira, A (2002). Reforming the Governance of the Bretton Wood Institutions, in The OPEC Fund for International Development (OPEC Fund), *Financing for Development*, Pamphlet Series 33, Vienna: 213–255.

Chirwa EW and Mlachila M (2004). Financial Reforms and Interest Rate Spreads in the Commercial Banking System in Malawi. *IMF Staff papers*, 51 (1). Washington, DC.

Chowdhury AR (2001). External Debt and Growth in Developing Countries, A Sensitivity and Causal Analysis. United Nations University/World Institute for Development Economics Research (UNU/WIDER) Discussion Paper No. 2001/95 (www.wider.unu.edu/publications/dps/dp2001-95.pdf).

Christensen J (2004). Domestic Debt Markets in Sub Saharan Africa. *IMF Working Paper* WP/04/46. Washington, DC.

Claessens S, Detragiache E, Kanbur R and Wickham P (1997). Analytical Aspects of the Debt Problems of Heavily Indebted Countries in Zubair Iqbal and Ravi Kanbur (eds), *External Finance for Low-Income Countries*: 21–48. IMF, Washington, DC.

Claessens S, Detragiache E, Kanbur R and Wickham P (1996). Analytical aspects of the Debt Problems of Heavily Indebted Poor Countries, *Policy Research Working Paper*, 1618, World Bank, Washington DC.

Clements B, Bhattacharya R and Nguyen TQ (2003). External Debt, Public Investment, and Growth in Low-Income Countries. *IMF Working Paper*, WP/03/249. (www.imf.org/external/pubs/ft/wp/2003/wp03249.pdf).

Cline W (1995). *International Debt Re-examined*, Institute for International Economics, Washington, DC.

Cline W (1997). "Debt Relief for Heavily Indebted Poor Countries: Lessons from the Debt Crisis of the 1980s", in Zubair, I. and Kanbur, R (eds), *External Finance for Low-income Countries*, pp. 134–144. IMF, Washington, DC.

Cohen, D (2003). Maintaining Debt Sustainability in the Future. Paper presented at the Joint IMF/World Bank Workshop on Debt Sustainability in Low Income Countries, Washington, DC, 11–12 September.

Dagdeviren H and Weeks J (2001). How Much Poverty could HIPC reduce? Paper presented at the WIDER Development Conference on debt relief, Helsinki, Finland, 17–18 August.

Daseking C and Powell R (1999), From Toronto Terms to the HIPC Initiative: A brief history of debt relief for low-income countries, *IMF Working Paper* 99/142, International Monetary Fund, Washington, DC.

Debt Relief International (2003). Critical Assessment of Existing Debt Proposal, A paper presented at the ECA Conference of Debt Experts, Dakar, 17 October.

Devarajan S, Swanson EV and Miller MJ (2002). Goals for Development: History, Prospects and Costs. Washington, DC, World Bank Working Paper 2819.

Dijkstra G and Hermes N (2001). The Uncertainty of Debt Service Payments and Economic Growth of HIPCs, Is there a Case for Debt Relief? United Nations University/World Institute for Development Economics Research (UNU/WIDER) Discussion Paper No. 2001/122 (www.wider.unu.edu/publications/dps/dp2001-122.pdf).

Dittus P (1989). The Budgetary Dimension of the Debt Crisis in Low-Income Sub-Saharan Countries, *Journal of Institutional and Theoretical Economics*, 145 (2), June: 358–366.

Dornbusch R (1985). Policy and Performance Links between LDC Debtors and Industrial Nations. *Brooking Papers of Economic Activity* (1985/1): 303–56.

Drummond J (2004). Rich Countries Should Agree on the Best Measure of a Poor Country's Debt is its Ability to Pay. *Financial Times*, 19 February 2004.

Easterly W (1999). How did Highly Indebted Poor Countries Become Highly Indebted? Reviewing Two Decades of Debt Relief, *World Bank Policy Research Working Paper* 2346, Washington, DC.

Edwards S (2002). *Debt Relief and Fiscal Sustainability*. National Bureau of Economic Research (NBER) Working Paper 8939. Cambridge, MA, USA.

Edwards S (2003). Debt Relief and the Current Account, An Analysis of the HIPC Initiative. *The World Economy* 26 (4): 513–31.

Edwards S and Savasatano M (2000). Exchange Rates in Emerging Economies: What Do We Know? What Do We Need to Know? In Krueger AO (ed) *Economic Policy Reform: The Second Stage*. University of Chicago Press, Chicago.

EURODAD (2002). Going the Extra Mile: How and why creditors should go further with debt reduction for the poorest countries. European Network on Debt and Development, Brussels.

Fedelino A, and Kudina A (2003). *Fiscal Sustainability in African HIPC Countries, A Policy Dilemma?* IMF Working Paper, WP/03/187 (www.imf.org/external/pubs/ft/wp/2003/wp03187.pdf).

General Accounting Office (GAO) (2000). *Developing Countries: Debt Relief Initiative for Poor Countries Facing Challenges*, United States General Accounting Office, Washington, DC.

General Accounting Office (GAO) (2004). *Achieving Poor Countries' Economic Growth and Debt Relief Targets Faces Significant Financing Challenges* (GAO-04-405), United States General Accounting Office, Washington, DC, April.

G-24 Secretariat (2003). Heavily Indebted Poor Country (HIPC) Initiative. G-24 Secretariat Briefing Paper 2, March.

Gautam, M. (2003). *The Heavily Indebted Poor Countries (HIPC) Debt Initiative, An OED Review*. World Bank, Operations Evaluation Department (OED). Washington, DC (www.worldbank.org/oed/).

George, S (1995). Excerpts from "Debt as warfare: An overview of the debt crisis", *Development and Socio-Economic Progress* No. 61, January-March.

Gunter, BG (2001). Does the HIPC Initiative Achieve its Goal of Debt Sustainability. United Nations University/World Institute for Development Economics Research (UNU/WIDER) Discussion Paper 2001/100 (September 2001) (www.wider.unu.edu/publications/dps/dp2001-100.pdf).

Gunter, BG (2002). What's Wrong with the HIPC Initiative and What's Next? *Development Policy Review* 20 (1): 5–24.

Gunter, BG(2003). Achieving Debt Sustainability in Heavily Indebted Poor Countries (HIPCs). In Ariel Buira (ed) *Challenges to the World Bank and IMF, Developing Country Perspectives*. London, Anthem Press: 91–117; summarized version of a paper presented at the 16th Technical Meeting of the Intergovernmental Group of 24 (G-24) in Trinidad, February 13–14, 2003 (www.g24.org/guntetgm.pdf).

Gunter, BG and Wodon Q (2004). The Impact of the HIPC Initiative on World Inequality. World Bank, Washington, DC, (mimeo, draft of February 2004).

Hansen H,k (2001). The Impact of Aid and External Debt on Growth and Investment, Insights from Cross-Country Regression Analysis. Paper presented at the United Nations University (UNU)/World Institute for Development Economics Research (WIDER) Development Conference on Debt Relief, Helsinki (www.wider.unu.edu/conference/conference-2001-2/parallel%20papers/2_1_Hansen.pdf).

Hjertholm P (1999). *Analytical History of Heavily Indebted Poor Country (HIPC) Debt Sustainability Targets*. Revised version of Paper prepared for the joint World Bank/Nordic Working Seminar: Review of the HIPC Initiative, Oslo, 4 March.

Hjertholm P (2003). Theoretical and Empirical Foundations of HIPC Debt Sustainability Targets, *Journal of Development Studies*, 39 (6), August: 67–100.

The Independent (2004), The Independent Newspaper Group, UK, 17 February.

IMF (1999). Measuring financial development in Sub Saharan Africa, *IMF Working Paper*, WP/99/05, Washington, DC.

IMF (2003a). *World Economic Outlook: Public Debt in Emerging Markets,* Washington, DC, September.

IMF (2003b). Debt Sustainability in Low-Income Countries — Towards a Forward-Looking Strategy. Washington, DC, 23 May.

IMF and World Bank (2001a). *The Challenge of Maintaining Long-Term External Debt Sustainability.* Washington, DC, 20 April.

IMF and World Bank (2001b). *Assistance to Post-Conflict Countries and the HIPC Framework.* Washington, DC, 20 April.

IMF and World Bank (2002a). *The Enhanced HIPC Initiative and the Achievement of Long-Term External Debt Sustainability.* Washington, DC, 15 April.

IMF and World Bank (2002b).). *Heavily Indebted Poor Countries (HIPC) Initiative, Status of Implementation.* Washington, DC, 23 September

IMF and World Bank (2003a). *Heavily Indebted Poor Countries (HIPC) Initiative, Status of Implementation.* Washington, DC, 12 September.

IMF and World Bank (2003b). *Republic of Uganda: Joint Staff Assessment of the Poverty Reduction Strategy Paper Annual Progress Report.* Washington DC, 13 August.

IMF and World Bank (2003c). *Poverty Reduction Strategy Papers – Progress in Implementation.* Washington DC, 12 September.

IMF and World Bank (2004a). *Global Monitoring Report 2004 – Policies and Actions for Achieving the MDGs and Related Outcomes.* Washington, DC, April.

IMF and World Bank (2004b). *Debt Sustainability in Low-Income Countries – Proposals for an Operational Framework and Policy Implications.* Washington, DC, 3 February.

Jubilee Research (2003). *HIPC: Real Progress Report on HIPC.* New Economics Foundation, London, UK, September.

Kane O (2003). External Shocks and Debt Sustainability in Low Income Countries, The Case of African HIPCs. Paper presented at the Joint IMF/World Bank Workshop on Debt Sustainability in Low Income Countries, Washington, DC, 11–12 September.

Killick T (2004). Politics, Evidence and the New Aid Agenda. *Development Policy Review* 22 (1), 5–29.

Kraay A and Nehru V (2003). When is Debt Sustainable? Paper presented at the IMF Research Workshop on Macroeconomic Challenges in Low Income Countries, IMF, Washington, DC, 23–24 October. (www.imf.org/external/np/res/seminars/2003/lic/pdf/kn.pdf).

Kuznets PW (1988). An East Asian Model of Economic Development: Japan, Taiwan and South Korea. Economic Development and Cultural Change 36 (3).

Loko B, Mlachila M, Nallari R and Kalonji K (2003). The Impact of External Indebtedness on Poverty in Low-Income Countries, IMF Working Paper, WP/03/61 (www.imf.org/external/pubs/ft/wp/2003/wp0361.pdf).

Martin M (2002). Debt Relief and Poverty Reduction: Do we need a HIPC III? Paper presented to North-South Institute, Global Finance Governance Initiative workshop, Ottawa, May 1–2.

Martin M and Alami R (2001). *Long-term Debt Sustainability for HIPCs: How to Respond to Shocks.* Debt Relief International, London.

Nafula N (2002). Achieving Sustainable Universal Primary Education through Debt Relief: The Case of Kenya, WIDER Discussion Paper, DP2002/66(July) www.wider.unu.edu/publications/publications.htm).

Ndikumana, L and Boyce JK (1998). Congo's Odious Debt: External Borrowing and Capital Flight in Zaire, *Development and Change*, Vol. 29: 195–217.

Northover H (2001). A Human Development Approach to Debt Relief for the World's Poor. CAFOD, London, UK. Available at www.cafod.org.uk/policy/acaf1.shtml.

Pattillo C, Poirson H, and Ricci L(2002). External Debt and Growth. *IMF Working Paper*, WP/02/69 (www.imf.org/external/pubs/ft/wp/2002/wp0269.pdf).

Reisen H (1987). *Über das Transferproblem hochverschuldeter Entwicklungsländer*. Baden-Baden., Germany.

Rwegasira DG and Mwega FM (2003). Public Debt and Macroeconomic Management in Sub-Saharan Africa, in UNCTAD (2003). *Management of Capital Flows: Comparative Experiences and Implications for Africa*, United Nations, New York and Geneva, April: 259–312.

Sachs, JD (2002). Resolving the Debt Crisis of Low-Income Countries. *Brookings Papers on Economic Activity*, 2002 (1): pp 257–86. The Brookings Institution, Washington, DC.

Sala-i-Martin X and Subramanian A (2003). Addressing the Natural Resource Curse: An Illustration from Nigeria, IMF Working Paper WP/03/139 ,July (www.imf.org/external/pubs/).

Sanford JE (2004a). IMF Gold and the World Bank's Unfunded HIPC Deficit. *Development Policy Review* 22 (1): 31–40.

Sanford JE (2004b). IDA Grants and HIPC Debt Forgiveness, Their Effectiveness and Impact on IDA Resources. *World Development* (forthcoming).

Serieux JE and Yiagadeesen S (2001). The Debt Service Burden and Growth, Evidence from Low-Income Countries. Paper presented at the United Nations University (UNU)/World Institute for Development Economics Research (WIDER) Development Conference on Debt Relief, Helsinki (www.wider.unu.edu/conference/conference-2001-2/parallel%20papers/4_2_Serieux.pdf).

United Nations (2000). Recent Developments in the Debt Situation of Developing Countries. Report of the Secretary-General, General Assembly, Fifty-fifth session, Agenda item 92 (c), Macroeconomic Policy Questions: External Debt Crisis and Development, A/55/422, New York, 26 September.

United Nations (2001). Report of the High-Level Panel on Financing for Development (Zedillo Report), A/55/1000. New York, 26 June,.

UNCTAD (1986). *Trade and Development Report, 1986*. United Nations publication, sales no. E.86. II.D.5, New York and Geneva.

UNCTAD (1996). *Trade and Development Report, 1996*. United Nations publication, sales no. E.96.II.D.6, New York and Geneva.

UNCTAD (1998). *Trade and Development Report, 1998*. United Nations publication, sales no. E.98.II.D.6, New York and Geneva.

UNCTAD (2000). *Capital Flows and Growth in Africa*. UNCTAD/GDS/MDPB/7, United Nations, New York and Geneva.

UNCTAD (2001). *Economic Development in Africa: Performance Prospects and Policy Issues*, UNCTAD/GDS/AFRICA/1, United Nations, New York and Geneva.

UNCTAD (2002a). *Economic Development in Africa: From adjustment to poverty reduction: What is new?* (UNCTAD/GDS/AFRICA/2).(Sales no. E.02.II.D.18) United Nations, New York and Geneva.

UNCTAD (2002b). *The Least Developed Countries Report, 2002*. United Nations publication, sales no. E.02.II.D.13, New York and Geneva.

UNCTAD (2003). *Economic Development in Africa: Trade Performance and Commodity Dependence* (UNCTAD/GDS/AFRICA/2003/1), sales no. E.03.II.D.34. United Nations, New York and Geneva.

Vasquez, I. (2001). Debt relief for poor countries: Are the World Bank and IMF doing the right thing? Cato Institute Policy Forum, July 16, Ian Vasquez (Moderator and Presenter), with Lerrick A., Galliot Center for Public Policy, Carnegie Mellon University; and Hadjimichael M, IMF, The Cato Institute, FA Hayek Auditorium, Washington, DC.

Were, M (2001). The Impact of External Debt on Economic Growth in Kenya, An Empirical Assessment. United Nations University/World Institute for Development Economics Research (UNU/WIDER) Discussion Paper No. 2001/116. (www.wider.unu.edu/publications/dps/dp2001-116.pdf).

World Bank (2000). A Strategy for Increasing IDA's Effectiveness in Africa, Africa Region, December.

World Bank (2002). *Global Development Finance*. Washington, DC.

World Bank (2003). *Global Development Finance: Striving for Stability in Development Finance*. Washington, DC.

World Bank (2004). The Poverty Reduction Strategy Initiative: An Independent Evaluation of the World Bank's Support Through 2003. World Bank Operations Evaluations Department, Washington, DC, July.

Other works consulted:

Abrego L and Ross DC (2001). *Debt Relief under the HIPC Initiative: Context and Outlook for Debt Sustainability and Resource Flow*. IMF Working Paper 144. Washington, DC.

Addison T, Hansen H, and Tarp F (eds) (forthcoming) *Debt Relief*. New York, Oxford University Press for UNU/WIDER.

Cohen D (1996). The Sustainability of African Debt. Policy Research Working Paper 1621, World Bank, Washington, DC.

Cuddington J (1997). *Analyzing the Sustainability of Fiscal Deficits in Developing Countries*. Policy Research Paper 1784., World Bank, Washington, DC.

Greenhill R and Sisti E (2003). Real Progress Report on HIPC, London, Jubilee Research at New Economic Foundation (NEF) in co-operation with CAFOD, Christian Aid, EURODAD and Oxfam (www.cafod.org.uk).

Hansen H (2001). The Impact of Aid and External Debt on Growth and Investment, Insights from Cross-Country Regression Analysis. Paper presented at the United Nations University (UNU)/World Institute for Development Economics Research (WIDER) Development Conference on Debt Relief, Helsinki (www.wider.unu.edu/conference/conference-2001-2/parallel%20papers/2_1_Hansen.pdf).

White H and Killick T (in collaboration with Kayizzi-Mugerwa S and Savane M-A) (2001). African poverty at the Millennium: Causes, Complexities and Challenges, World Bank, Washington, DC.

World Bank (2004). *Global Monitoring Report 2004*, Washington, DC.